Elgin Community College Library
Elgin, IL 60123

Career Launcher

Energy

Career Launcher series

Career Launcher

Energy

Kelly Kagamas Tomkies

An Infobase Learning Company

Elgin Community College
Library

331.7621
Tᴜ58e

Career Launcher: **Energy**

Copyright © 2011 by Infobase Learning, Inc.

All rights reserved. No part of this book may be reproduced or utilized in any form or by any means, electronic or mechanical, including photocopying, recording, or by any information storage or retrieval systems, without permission in writing from the publisher. For information contact:

Ferguson's
An imprint of Infobase Learning
132 West 31st Street
New York NY 10001

Library of Congress Cataloging-in-Publication Data

Tomkies, Kelly Kagamas.
    Energy / by Kelly Kagamas Tomkies.
        p. cm.—(Career launcher)
    Includes bibliographical references and index.
    ISBN-13: 978-0-8160-7957-5 (hardcover : alk. paper)
    ISBN-10: 0-8160-7957-9 (hardcover : alk. paper)
 1. Energy industries—Vocational guidance—Juvenile literature. I. Title.
    TJ163.23.T645 2011
    333.79023—dc23

                                           2011013994

Ferguson's books are available at special discounts when purchased in bulk quantities for businesses, associations, institutions, or sales promotions. Please call our Special Sales Department in New York at (212) 967-8800 or (800) 322-8755.

You can find Ferguson's on the World Wide Web at
http://www.infobaselearning.com

Produced by Print Matters, Inc.
Text design by A Good Thing, Inc.
Cover design by Takeshi Takahashi
Cover printed by Yurchak Printing, Landisville, Pa.
Book printed and bound by Yurchak Printing, Landisville, Pa.
Date printed: October 2011

Printed in the United States of America

10 9 8 7 6 5 4 3 2 1

This book is printed on acid-free paper.

Contents

Foreword

There could not be a better time to work in the energy industry. Why? Baby boomers are retiring in record numbers causing a shortage of talent that is desperately needed to help utilities balance the increasing demand for energy with growing concerns over climate change. Energy organizations are now working on succession planning and training programs to slow down the "brain drain" of industry knowledge caused by the mass exodus of retiring employees.

In addition to an aging workforce, the energy efficiency and demand management segment of the industry is expanding as more utilities increase their spending on energy efficiency programs. According to the Consortium for Energy Efficiency (CEE), U.S. utilities increased their spending on energy efficiency programs by 43 percent in 2009, for a total expenditure of $5.3 billion. This kind of spending, coupled with an aging workforce, means opportunities are opening in nearly every part of the energy industry. Our industry needs the best and brightest to help us meet the challenges of a growing demand for electricity.

Personally speaking, I have found my 30 years (and counting) in the energy industry to be challenging and rewarding. As someone who has worked for an investor-owned utility, held several positions with consulting firms, and is now working in the nonprofit sector, I can say that my career has definitely taken unexpected twists and turns resulting in positions that have taught me a lot and allowed me the opportunity to teach others.

As you review the pages of this book and discover the many career opportunities the energy industry offers, remember that new positions will be created as we work to solve the country's need to reduce its dependence on foreign oil, develop the Smart Grid to help customers better manage their energy use, and create green jobs centered on renewable forms of energy.

We energy professionals are passionate about the work we do. We dedicate our lives to not only keeping the lights on and the burner tips lit, but to also gain a deeper understanding of what is important to our customers. After all, everyone needs water and power to live, and energy providers are spending more than ever to understand the needs and wants of their customers by using sophisticated research tools and the latest channels of communication.

If you do choose a career in energy, remember to invest in developing a strong professional network of people who will mentor you and help you reach your highest level of success. Developing relationships with people who can help you along the way is the secret to success!

Enjoy the journey.

—Meg Matt, President and CEO
ASSOCIATION OF ENERGY SERVICE PROFESSIONALS,
PHOENIX, ARIZONA

Acknowledgments

I would like to thank Richard Rothschild of Print Matters, as well as my husband, Kevin, my daughter, Tya, and my son, Duncan. Without the support of all of them, I couldn't have completed the writing of this book.

Introduction

Perhaps more than any other industry, the energy sector has a direct and immediate effect on every aspect of our lives and livelihood. It is the cog that drives all other aspects of 21st century existence—fuel for our automobiles, power for our factories, heat for our homes, refrigeration for our food, and connectivity for our computers, among other things. Energy related industries employ 2.7 million men and women in skilled professions, and account for nearly 7 percent of the U.S. economy and 2 percent of its workforce. Even a small fluctuation in the price of oil can have a major impact on the stock market, interest rates, food production, transportation—nearly every sector of the world economy.

There are many extreme examples of energy-related crises that have affected millions, if not billions of people, businesses, and governments. Whether they are caused by something as major as a government's decision to support one side over another in a war, or something as simple as a failure to properly trim a stand of trees, they can still wreak havoc on everything from a local to an international scale. For example, in 1973, an oil embargo spurred by the Yom Kippur War caused crude oil prices to jump from $3 a barrel to $12 a barrel in less than a year. Not only did the embargo lead to long lines at the pump and panic about the availability of gasoline, it helped contribute to worldwide inflation and recession. On August 14, 2003, sagging high-voltage power lines brushed against overgrown trees in northern Ohio, causing a cascading event across the northeastern power grid that led to power failures through southeastern Canada and eight northeastern states. More than 50 million people lost power for two days in the worst blackout in North American history. The event, which cost an estimated $6 billion dollars and contributed to at least eleven deaths, has led to efforts to reinvent how not only how electricity is created, but how it is delivered.

In addition to its influence on other industries and the world economy, the energy industry has a profound effect on the environment. It generates a large amount of pollution, including toxic and greenhouse gases, nuclear waste, and coal ash. The harvesting and collection of energy—from mountaintop removal and strip mining to the construction of vast wind farms—permanently alters the landscape. Due to government and industry regulations, an increasing part of doing business in the energy sector involves trading carbon and pollution credits as well as developing new state-of-the-art pollution control measures.

The energy industry has always been extremely complicated; however, the myriad issues the sector faces in the 21st century make it even more difficult to understand. Energy sector jobs cover a wide variety of professions ranging from those that require little college education—construction trades, extraction workers, linesmen, pipe fitters, plumbers, and steamfitters—to the highly specialized fields of electrical and chemical engineers, environmental scientists, and geoscientists. According to the U.S. Bureau of Labor Statistics, jobs in the scientific and technical consulting services are projected to be among the highest in salary increases over the next ten years. Ninety percent of the jobs in the energy sector are blue collar or technical positions. This book will focus on these as well as the business-related segment of the energy employment picture.

Generally speaking, the energy sector produces, refines, and distributes fuels for propulsion, heat, and light. These fuels include oil, natural gas, electricity, coal, wind, water, sunlight, and nuclear. Traditionally, the industry has been divided between the oil and gas sector and the electricity sector, each accounting for about half of the industry as a whole. The oil and gas industry consists of the exploration for, and the extraction, refinement, and distribution of oil and natural gas. Electricity is the business of converting fuels such as natural gas, coal, nuclear, wind, water, and solar to electricity and then distributing that electricity to customers via an intricate interconnected network of power grids. Most professionals enter either oil and natural gas or electricity, with rare crossovers between the two sectors. Natural gas is one industry that intersects the two, as it is collected along with oil despite being used to generate electricity.

Career Launcher: Energy breaks down this often complicated industry into its most basic components and provides vital information for those looking to enter the field on a professional level. Divided into six chapters, it can be read either front to back for a concise, overall snapshot, or used as a fingertip reference to cull specific pieces of information.

While no book can encapsulate everything you need to know about a particular industry, the goal of this book is to put together a package of information that will give you a historical perspective, key trends, a snapshot of the industry, an idea of the many job opportunities available, and provide you with tips for success and resources you can use throughout your career. Whether you just graduated from college or technical school or are starting out as a linesman or customer service rep for a utility company, you will have lots of questions. *Career Launcher: Energy* may not have *all* the answers, but you will find this book loaded with enough information that if you cannot find the answers in its pages, you will definitely know where to go to find it outside of them.

In brief, Chapter 1 is a succinct history of the energy industry from its earliest days to the present. It covers the industry's origins: the people, companies, and politics that have shaped its path and drive its future.

Chapter 2 studies the current state of the industry and the issues that shape it today. There is information on trends in employment and wages, an examination of the different types of companies (oil companies, utilities, energy service firms, transmission grid operators, consulting firms, government agencies, and nonprofits, among others), an overview of the regulatory environment and how it impacts the industry, and an overview of the major players in energy, including ExxonMobil, Occidental Petroleum, MidAmerican Energy Holdings, Halliburton, and American Electric Power. Also in Chapter 2 is an overview of major industry conferences and organizations.

Chapter 3 provides a detailed, alphabetical listing of key jobs and positions within the various segments of the energy industry. It examines the various employment areas, including financial, consulting, energy services, engineering, mining and exploration, power marketing and research utilities, as well as the job categories within each of these areas—administrative, analytics, economics, management, technician, marketing, customer service, engineering, sales, and trading. Each job description will include whether it is considered an entry level, midlevel, or executive level position; the education and training needed to obtain it; whether the position includes supervising others; and what the opportunities are for promotion. By understanding the overall employment picture of this complex industry and how these different positions interact with one another, the reader will be better equipped to define a career path and identify areas for advancement.

Chapter 4 offers "Tips for Success" in the energy industry: identifying your skill sets and matching them to your ideal job; preparing for and completing a successful interview; and, once you are hired, developing a professional reputation, managing your time, and achieving success in the energy industry. This chapter goes far beyond the basics to provide in-depth strategies that will help you succeed in your chosen area of expertise, whether you are working for a large energy conglomerate, a small issue-related nonprofit, or a heavily regulated utility. Some successful career paths are sparked by finding that ideal position working with a professional mentor who will help guide you through the ins and outs of successful collaboration. Others depend more on self-direction and the continual development of your skills through education, training, and certification.

Chapter 5 offers an in-depth guide to industry jargon, key terminology, industry-specific phrases and concepts, and general business terms. Much of this jargon and terminology crosses over to other professions and career paths; however, the energy sector utilizes a more specific language than many other industries and professions. This chapter will help you to talk like a knowledgeable professional. By learning and understanding this language, you will be better equipped to discuss these difficult concepts with the layman and the expert alike.

To fully understand the complicated business of energy, you will need to go outside these pages to continue your education and knowledge. Chapter 6 identifies key publications, Web sites, books, schools, trade organizations, and associations and training programs that are relevant to anyone working in the energy industry today. In order to move ahead and succeed in any industry, you must continually educate yourself about current and ever-changing trends and issues facing your industry.

Throughout each chapter are the following sidebars, which contain quick capsules of helpful information and advice:

- ➡ **Best Practices** provide tips on improving your efficiency and performance in the workplace. Some are aimed specifically at the energy industry; others apply to careers in general.
- ➡ **Everyone Knows** provide crucial information that everyone entering the energy industry should understand.
- ➡ **Fast Facts** are handy nuggets of information that will impress colleagues and interviewers. These are fun, useful tidbits that will help you stand out from the crowd, as well as give you important facts and statistics about the industry.

➜ **Keeping in Touch** provide ideas for effective business communication and professionalism. Included here are tips for successful communication through e-mail, phone, in person, and during meetings and interviews, as well as strategies for successful networking.

➜ **On the Cutting Edge** discuss emerging trends, concerns and challenges and examine the state-of-the-art technology present in the energy industry today. Included here are many of the recent and future developments in alternative energies, conservation, modernization, pollution control, and dependency.

➜ **Problem Solving** examines actual and hypothetical problems faced by people in the energy industry, and offers resolution strategies and possible solutions.

➜ **Professional Ethics** show how ethical conduct is a necessity to building a strong career. They contain descriptions of ethical dilemmas specific to the energy industry and their successful resolutions.

We have designed *Career Launcher: Energy* to be both companion and advisor in your journey through the energy industry. Whether you are launching a new career, moving up the industry ladder, or looking to blaze a new career path, the tips, knowledge, strategies, and advice in these pages will provide the tools needed for realizing your career goals.

You will also learn a great deal about this industry: its strengths, its challenges, and how all of these are contributing to an exciting future. There are many opportunities that lay ahead for employees in the energy industry. And for dedicated professionals armed with a passion for their career and knowledge of their industry gained from reading this book and exploring other resources, you will be prepared to take advantage of all the energy industry has to offer.

Chapter 1

Industry History

When most people think of the subject of history, they think of memorizing dates and names. The subject itself seems dull and boring—without life. When it comes to learning all you can about your chosen field, however, reading about its history can serve some very important purposes. For example, the phrase "History always repeats itself" is not without some elements of truth. Employees have ideas that can improve a company's standing in the market or efficiency in transmission or delivery. There is a good chance that someone in the past has tried a similar idea. Knowing the history of what worked and what did not, and especially *why*, can save everyone the grief of launching an idea that has already failed many times in the past. It can also inspire employees to think of innovative ways to customize that idea so that it will work.

Another important reason to read up on industry history is to understand its trends. Unless you have years of experience in the industry, studying its history is the next best way to pick up on important trends. How long have Americans been concerned with conserving energy and why? Will that trend continue? Are consumers turning more frequently to alternative fuel and energy sources? These are questions that learning industry history can help answer.

Lastly, just learning how we got to the point where we are now—when Americans are consuming the greatest amount of power in our history—is an interesting story. From ancient times when energy meant lighting a fire to the arrival of superconductors, this history will depict the energy industry's evolution, which is still very far from over. The difference will be the new employees who can change the future of the industry.

Energy Use in Ancient History

From humankind's earliest days, the need for energy has driven us to develop some of our most important inventions, from the steam engine to the light bulb and today's green energy alternatives. The drive to possess the fuels to create energy has also created a great deal of conflict. Everyone needs energy for just about everything we do each day. As the world's population grows, so does its energy needs.

Early in our history, people used the sun and fire for energy, mainly for keeping warm and cooking. They also used fire to protect them from attacks from hungry animals. Historians have stated that early humans learned to control fire as early as 1 million B.C.E. The next energy sources to be tapped in history were wind and water. As early as 1200 B.C.E., natives of Polynesia learned how to use wind to propel their sail boats. The ancient Greeks harnessed hydropower more than 2000 years ago, using water wheels to grind grains. The use of waterwheels spread quickly throughout Europe, and soon these energy sources—muscle, water, and wind—were dominating world culture and did so for many years. Eventually they took the form of axes, picks, plows, harnesses, wagons and carriages, water-wheels, windmills, and sailing ships. By the end of the Roman era, countries with plentiful water sources had converted its power into an energy source: waterwheels powered mills to crush grain, tan leather, smelt and shape iron, saw wood, and carry out a variety of other early industrial processes. Thanks to the use of this energy, productivity increased. The dependence on human and animal muscle power eventually lessened, and as they did so, places with good water power resources became centers of economic and indus-trial activity.

Energy in the Middle Ages: Hydropower

The first interesting development that occurred during the Middle Ages was the invention of the hydropower dam. By this time there were hydraulic engineers, who engineered a way to mount mills on boats and bridges. From these, hydropower dams evolved. They were used to store and develop water pressure and to divert water into power canals, and from there onto the waterwheels.

By the 15th century, industries, in the form of large milling facilities, had come to depend on water power for energy. Thanks to the inventions of the camshaft and crankshaft, water power could be applied to repetitive tasks, revolutionizing the iron industry. Because of these developments, the number of watermills in Europe continued to grow. Engineers continued to design and create large water powered industrial complexes, and by the 1770s, in England, large water powered cotton mills were operated by William Strutt and Richard Arkwright.

Around this time, the use of wind power enabled the first ships to sail across the ocean to America. The new colonists brought their water powered mills know-how with them, and soon these mills were popping up everywhere from Latin America to Canada. After the mill, textile factories developed and by 1820, large, water powered, industrial cities were created, generally in New England. The industrial revolution was primarily powered by water.

Energy During the Days of the Industrial Revolution: Steam Power

The next innovation in energy production was the introduction of steam as a source of energy. In the 18th century, Thomas Savery and Thomas Newcomen used steam power in English coal mines for pumps. These engines, as well as James Watt's version, replaced water-powered mine pumps. The two primary industries of the day—coal mining and iron—led to improvements in steam technology, and steam engines soon replaced waterwheels when it came to powering English textile mills. The main advantage of steam was that it could be used anywhere, as opposed to water energy, which required a nearby water source. Still, water power continued to be used throughout much of the 19th century until steam power's flexibility and affordability won out over water power.

One reason that the invention of the steam engine was so important to the energy industry is that it required wood or coal to create the steam, and by the mid-19th century, coal had become the fuel of choice. Countries in Europe led the transition to coal, but in America it was solidified by the development of ample coal mines in the Appalachian United States. Manufacturers on the Pacific Coast still used wood, but coal was preferred. Coal was scarce on the Western coast, though, but petroleum was not. Once petroleum was discovered it replaced both wood and coal as fuel for steam until a much later period of time.

It was during this time, in the throes of the industrial revolution, that the demand for energy increased at a remarkable rate, primarily due to the creation of factories and mass production of various products. Once the products were created, they needed to be shipped, creating more demand for transportation fuel. Steamboats and trains were the earliest preferred methods of transportation driving energy demand. Even in these early days, scientists were becoming concerned about the exhaust fumes that were derived from coal and petroleum use. This led them to start developing natural energy sources as an alternative to coal. The energy sources include solar energy, hydroelectric energy, and geothermal energy.

Fast Facts

Changing Statistics

Cars grew larger and heavier throughout the 1950s and 1960s. By 1970, the average mileage of an American car was only 13.5 miles per gallon, and a gallon of gas cost less than a quarter.

By midcentury, coal replaced wood as the preferred fuel in America's cities. In 1840, coal output reached a million tons, and in just 10 years that number quadrupled to four million tons. Coal was used in blast furnaces, in steam engines, and in making coal-gas for illumination. Natural gas was also tapped as a fuel for lighting during this period, although in a very limited way.

Still, despite the advent of fossil fuels, muscle power remained an important source of energy, particularly on the American farm, as mechanical innovations such as the cotton gin and the mechanical reaper made human and animal muscle power more productive. As a result, the use of steam-powered engines in farming did not surpass work animals until the later decades of the century.

Demand of coal rose dramatically as the country expanded westward, along with the railroads. As railroads drove west to the plains and the mountains, wood became less abundant, and plentiful coal deposits were found near the rail lines. In addition to its availability, coal had the advantage of a higher energy content, which increased the range and power of steam-driven trains. In addition, coal provided an economical source of coke for the production of the steel and iron used for rails and spikes.

It was also during this time that the first uses of petroleum were created. In the 18th century petroleum began to be used for lighting and as an ingredient in medicines, and then eventually as a heating fuel. The major milestone for petroleum came with the 1901 discovery of the Spindletop Oil Field Petroleum near Beaumont, Texas, followed by the advent of mass-produced automobiles.

The Invention of Electricity

The industrial revolution was powered by steam, but meanwhile scientists were making progress in the area of electricity. It was the production of electricity with primary batteries and then with electromagnetic induction, and the transmission of electricity through copper wires and the development of electric motors that created the modern transmission of power, especially over long distances.

By the end of the 19th century, machinery powered by electricity had replaced waterwheels, windmills, and steam engines. Even in these early days, electricity was generated and transmitted by hydroelectric and steam turbine power plants. This development meant that factories could be located anywhere. When it came to transportation, electric trolleys soon replaced horse-drawn buggies and steam-powered streetcars. Electricity also replaced outdoor gas lighting, and wood and coal stoves and heaters in homes. Rivers that had once turned waterwheels to grind corn were now grinding out electricity instead.

Thomas Edison is given the lion's share of the credit for the invention of electricity. It was Edison's invention of the incandescent lamp in the 1880s that made indoor lighting possible. He also created the first central generating system on Pearl Street in lower Manhattan, which became the model for other power generating and distribution facilities. Another important accomplishment of Edison's is his mentoring of other researchers who subsequently made important contributions to the development of electricity. A few of them include Frank Sprague, who developed the first successful electric street rail system in Richmond, Virginia, in 1887, and Nicola Tesla, who developed AC or alternating current power.

Edison's power system was called direct current (DC) and it became the standard for distributed electricity. The DC system generated and distributed electricity used by electric railways, manufacturing facilities, and lighting. Its prime drawback was that it could not be distributed over long distances. Tesla's AC system could, and soon customers at great distances from the generating plants could receive electricity. In 1888 George Westinghouse bought the patents from Tesla and took advantage of alternating power to build a power system for a gold mine in Telluride, Colorado. He followed that in 1895 with the world's first commercial system to produce and transmit alternating current electricity, the Ames Hydroelectric Generating Plant near Ophir, Colorado, and the original Niagara Falls Adams Power Plant. While electric generating plants were primarily fueled by water power well into the 20th century, coal-powered electric plants eventually overtook hydroelectric plants.

Electricity rapidly became the energy choice of the world. Researchers and scientists continuously worked together to find new applications for it. Edison's invention of the industrial research laboratory led to the creation of the General Electric Research Laboratory, which became a model for many scientists. At this lab, researchers improved the ways we could apply electricity. One of these researchers was William Coolidge, who developed a tungsten filament for Edison's incandescent lamp, and later the x-ray tube.

Despite the fact that a great deal of focus is turning to renewable energy sources, research continues to find more efficient ways to conduct electricity. In 1986, physicists Karl Müller and Johannes Bednorz were able to achieve superconductivity in lanthanum barium copper oxide (LBCO) at a temperature of 35K. Superconductivity creates a condition in which electricity can flow without resistance or loss of energy. In 2010 companies such as Consolidated Edison and American Superconductor have begun to use superconducting materials for the transmission of electricity. Using superconductors for the transmission of high loads of electricity reduces the waste of electricity by more than half.

The Invention of the Automobile

By the late 1800s, in addition to electricity, a new form of fuel was catching on: petroleum. Colonel Edwin Drake was the first person to drill and extract crude petroleum oil out of the ground in Titusville, Pennsylvania. This pesky stuff was always getting into drinking water wells and con men bottled it and sold it as medicine. When the whale oil industry took a nosedive, people started using petroleum in its place, mainly for lighting. It was discovered that several useful products could be produced from petroleum, including kerosene (a gas that was ideal for lighting purposes) and gasoline (a fuel that could be used for transportation).

Concurrent to the development of the petroleum industry was the development of the automobile, an invention that would come to have a huge impact on the energy industry as a whole. The first step toward the invention of the automobile was the French inventor J. J. Etienne Lenoir's creation of an internal combustion engine that used gasoline for fuel. The next step was completed by the German inventors Gottlieb Daimler and Karl Benz, who mounted an engine on a carriage. At about the same time, the Wright brothers invented the first airplane with a gasoline engine, and an era of faster and cheaper transportation had begun.

As automobiles became more prevalent, the need for fuel to power them increased dramatically. Since gasoline was the fuel that powered the internal combustion engine, petroleum began to overtake coal as the dominant energy source. Previously, cars used steam or electricity for power, but these could not sustain the energy needed to drive longer distances, which at the time meant 25 to 30 miles or more. Despite these developments, most people could not afford an automobile until Henry Ford created his assembly line method for manufacturing them. Ford used this method to create his Model T car in 1913, which was assembled in just over 90 minutes. In less than 15 years, the first Ford factory had produced 15 million cars.

As mentioned earlier, it is interesting to note that there were also electric cars around this time, which were preferred by many women. They were quiet, clean, and started without the hand crank used by gasoline-powered cars. However, these women had to admit that the gasoline cars could get them farther. Another interesting note is that in 1925 Ford created a car that could run on ethanol alcohol made from a hemp plant, and predicted that using this would be the fuel of the future. However, petroleum became the fuel most used due to its lower cost to produce and buy. It is estimated that the United States today consumes more than 21 million barrels of gasoline every day.

The Development of Nuclear Energy

With widespread use of electricity during the 20th century, the exploitation of energy resources increased dramatically. Hydroelectricity still played a large role, but water power sites that were easily accessible were soon tapped. To make the most of what they had, engineers improved steam turbine technology so that more electricity could be generated with smaller quantities of fuel. Steam turbines were first created by British engineer Charles Algernon Parsons in 1884. Water was heated to create compounded steam that turned a dynamo (a turbine that turns at very fast speeds) at 18,000 revolutions a minute. This led to power plants that were larger but more efficient, which lowered the price of the electricity they generated. In turn, this drop in price created an increase in the use of electricity. Electric generating plants used coal then oil as fuel to generate electricity.

By the 1960s, engineers had made generating facilities as efficient as possible with the technology they had, so the cost of electricity began to climb. At the same time, researchers concerned with acid rain and other negative environmental occurrences felt the use of fossil fuels was causing them. The search for an alternative to fossil fuel electric power generation began.

The origins of this search can be traced back to the late 1890s, when Marie Curie's work on new compounds led to the discoveries of radiation, atomic structure, and the power of the atom. Much work continued in this are in the early years of the 20th century, especially in Europe. It was Italian physicist Enrico Fermi who produced artificial radiation by bombing uranium atoms with neutrons in the 1930s. After moving with his family to the United States in 1938 due to increasing instability in Europe with the rise of Nazi Germany, Fermi took a professorship at Columbia University. In the early days of World War II, he discovered that a uranium atom split by a neutron would cause a chain reaction of atom splitting that would release enormous energy. The process was called nuclear fission, and Fermi and fellow Columbia University scientists as well as Albert Einstein persuaded the U.S. Government to study the idea because of its military implications. In 1942 President Franklin Roosevelt agreed to let these scientists study nuclear fission and its possibilities as military weapons. It was called the Manhattan Project, and was relocated to the University of Chicago. This work led to the development of the atomic bomb, which was dropped on Nagasaki and Hiroshima, both in Japan, in 1945.

After World War II the United States created an Atomic Energy Commission (AEC) to oversee nuclear weapons development and create nonmilitary applications of atomic energy. By the 1950s the AEC worked with public utilities to develop electric power

Fast

Facts

The Top 10 Largest Electric Public Power Utilities by Revenue, 2008

1. Puerto Rico Electric Power Authority, Puerto Rico: $4,592,787

2. Long Island Power Authority, New York: $3,615,563

3. Salt River Project, Arizona: $2,975,658

4. Los Angeles Department of Water & Power, California: $2,745,135

5. New York Power Authority, New York: $2,744,000

6. CPS Energy, Texas: $1,860,801

7. Santee Cooper, South Carolina: $1,568,618

8. JEA, Florida: $1,394,724

9. Sacramento Municipal Utility District, California: $1,321,834

10. Lower Colorado River Authority, Texas: $1,263,442

Data courtesy of the American Public Power Association.

generation using nuclear fission. It was not long before many people felt nuclear energy was the solution to the world's energy problem. Nuclear power plants were constructed across the country.

Westinghouse Electric Corporation designed the first fully commercial nuclear power plant, Yankee Rowe, which started up in 1960 and operated until 1992. At the same time, the Argonne National Laboratory developed the boiling water reactor (BWR); the first one, known as Dresden-1 and with the power to generate 250 megawatts (MWe), was designed by General Electric and started up in 1960. The BWR works by using nuclear energy to heat water. The heated water becomes steam, which drives a turbine. It is the motion of the turbine that creates energy. By the end of the decade, orders were being placed for pressurized water reactor (PWR) units and BWR reactor units of more than 1,000 MWe. A PWR works in the same way as a BWR, with one exception. The PWR does not allow the

---

INTERVIEW

Utilities Are a Necessity

Mark Crisson
CEO, American Public Power Association

What is the overall state of the energy industry? Would you say it is healthy, growing, or holding its own?

Our barometer is credit ratings. The three major ratings come from Moody's, Standard and Poors, and Fitch. Any utility company that borrows money receives a rating from these companies. By and large, the credit ratings for utilities are very good. Public power utilities are rated better than investor owned utilities. Ninety-eight percent of the public power utility systems have a stable outlook. Eighty percent of IOUs have a stable outlook. Utilities are a necessity. We always have a steady stream of income. The year 2009 was not a good year for the economy or for us. However, it was only the second year since World War II that total loads went down. In 2010 we saw a lot of load come back. Most of the load we lost had been industrial.

What are some of the issues that are impacting the industry and what kind of impacts are they having?

Probably the biggest issue is the uncertainty in the industry. We are a very heavily regulated industry and there has been significant additional regulations added that are causing some uncertainly. Some provisions under the Clean Air Act are causing significant investments by coal plants into reducing their emissions. This means the cost of coal is going to go up. Coal provides the fuel for generating electricity in half the country, so we're looking at a significant cost impact.

The EPA has been charged to do something about carbon emissions. The utility industry is already the most capital-intensive industry there is. We spend more dollars in capital per customer than any other industry. There is concern about how these environmental requirements will affect the industry. Most of the infrastructure lasts 25 to 30 years, so making decisions that could be impacted in the future are causing some anxiety.

These issues are also affecting hiring decisions. People who specialize in the environmental area, like biologists, will be in more demand. Learning all of the environmental regulations and EPA standards is clearly an area that requires strong competencies and skills. Evaluating the environmental landscape is one of the biggest areas for hiring and will continue to be so for awhile.

Another issue is the increased competition for fuels. In the next several decades energy costs will be much higher. Oil tends to impact them all, and the price of oil is expected to go up. Natural gas is a little better when it comes to price, but that depends on demand. Most new power plants that will be built in the future will use natural gas. There are some plants under construction that use coal, but there will be no new coal plants.

What do you see as future trends in the industry?

We will see a real transformation in how we interact with customers due to changing technology. The electric system is one big synchronous machine. The new meters allow interaction. Smart readers automatically read the meter and there is remote control of the meter. Jobs that involved physically going to the meter will no longer be necessary. For example, we won't have to send out a service person to shut off a customer at the meter for nonpayment, and turn the meter back on after receiving payment. It will all be done remotely. A lot of things will be done automatically. There will no longer be the need for meter readers. It will save millions of dollars.

Another trend we see is that the workforce is aging. The average age in the utility industry is well above the average for other industries. It's almost 50. We're looking at senior managers and top people eligible to retire in three to four years. It's a brain drain. The good news there is that it opens up opportunities for existing employees to move up and new people to become employed.

What advice would you give someone who is interested in pursuing a career with a public utility?

There are advantages to working in the industry. It's stable and we're not as affected by the economy as other industries. There have been a lot of increased technology improvements, which have led to an increase in automation. One thing we have to do is integrate alternative sources to give us flexibility with the resources that come on and off (solar energy stops when the sun goes down). New employees that can focus on these technologies as well as information systems or information technology will be in demand.

Even if you don't have a college degree there is a lot of job satisfaction in the other jobs available. There is a good living to be had with line work. If you don't want to be inside all day, line workers make good money. The traditional pensions they used to receive have been phased out, but the benefits are still pretty darn good.

water to boil. This allows most of the radioactivity to remain in the reactor area. Today 60 percent of the world capacity is PWR and 21 percent BWR.

Other countries, such as France, the Soviet Union, and other Eastern European countries all developed their own nuclear power facilities between 1956 and 1973. Around the world, with few exceptions, countries have chosen light water designs for their nuclear power programs. Canadian reactor development uses natural uranium fuel and heavy water as a moderator and coolant. Both heavy water and uranium fuel need to be used together for the system to work. Heavy water is a highly efficient compound called deuterium oxide. Its efficiency is caused by its low neutron absorption. This leads to the chain reaction in the reactor with natural uranium fuel. The first unit started up in 1962 and continues to be refined.

The United Kingdom also embraced nuclear energy early on. The first two nuclear power plants were opened in Great Britain in 1956. Although the country experienced the world's first nuclear accident in 1957, Prime Minister Harold Macmillan kept the details from becoming public knowledge. It was later learned that a fire in the reactor caused the release of radioactivity. Between 1962 and 1986, seven nuclear power stations and 10 PWRs were constructed in the United Kingdom. After the nuclear event at Chernobyl, the country decided to privatize nuclear energy generation. However, no new plants were built, and no private companies wished to take over ownership and maintenance of the plants. Since 2000, the United Kingdom's nuclear energy system has not fared well, with government scandals over falsified safety reports. It was not until 2006 that Prime Minister Tony Blair endorsed the planning of new nuclear power generating stations. In 2008, a lack of skilled nuclear engineers halted the development of eight new nuclear power plants in the United Kingdom. However, plans are still being discussed for new plants to be constructed.

The United States has had its own struggles with the advent of nuclear power. By the end of the 1970s, there was quite a bit of concern about nuclear power in California in relation to earthquakes. For this reason, no new nuclear power plants were to be built there. In 1979 a partial core meltdown in a nuclear reactor at the Three Mile Island nuclear power plant in Pennsylvania caused the release of large amounts of nuclear reactor coolant into the surrounding area. Similarly, the 1986 meltdown at the Chernobyl nuclear power plant in the Ukraine and the radiation poisoning that resulted led many countries, including Italy and Germany, to look at other energy sources. The accident at Three Mile Island was just one in a long line of problems plaguing the nuclear industry. New plant orders had already ceased because of multibillion-dollar cost overruns, high inflation, and a slowdown in electricity demand growth due to the early effects of energy conservation.

Since the birth of the new century, several factors have combined to create a new interest in nuclear power use for energy. First, the reality of an increase in the demand for power worldwide is a matter of growing concern. Much of this increased demand will be created by currently underdeveloped countries quickly changing and developing. These nations want to use greener, more efficient, and renewable energy sources rather than dirty, nonrenewable fossil fuels. This could lead to higher job growth both in the United States and abroad, as the United States seeks to assist developing countries as they produce energy.

Other concerns include energy security and the need to limit carbon emissions due to worries about global warming. These factors, combined with the availability of a new generation of nuclear power reactors, have created an increasing demand for nuclear power. Finland and France are the two countries that ordered PWR plants in 2004. In the United States, the 2005 Energy Policy Act provided incentives and reimbursements for establishing new generation power reactors in the country. However, these efforts are much smaller than those recently going on in China, India, Japan, and South Korea. By 2020, China will have six times its current nuclear power capacity, and has more than 100 large units proposed and backed by political and popular support. A large portion of these are the latest Western design, expedited by modular construction. The tragedy of Japan's flooded nuclear reactors in 2011, however, remains a terrible reminder of the ever-present dangers of nuclear power.

The Introduction and History of Solar Energy

The first machine that created solar energy was developed by French inventor Auguste Mouchout in 1860. He used a glass-enclosed iron cauldron and reflectors that concentrated the solar radiation, heating the water in the cauldron until it boiled. The steam the water produced operated a small engine. Other scientists, like William Adams, observed Mouchout's invention and sought to improve it by adding mirrors. By using 72 mirrors, Adams's machine produced three times the power of Mouchout's. Other modifications were subsequently introduced by scientists Charles Tellier, John Ericsson, Henry E. Willsie, and others. These engines did not catch on because they were much more expensive to build than engines that used coal.

At the same time solar energy was being developed, other alternative energy sources were being harnessed. Small hydroelectric power plants were constructed; people began using windmills for electricity; and geothermal energy was used to heat houses and, by the end of the century, to produce electricity. The first commercial solar cell was made available to the public at a very expensive $300 per watt in the early 1950s. Today it is used in radios and toys. It was also in the 1950s that space programs began using solar technologies. In 1958, the Vanguard I was launched. It was the first satellite that used solar energy to generate electricity.

In the 1970s, the energy crisis sparked interest in alternative fuel sources. Suddenly it became important to find an alternative form of energy as people realized just how reliant the United States (as well as other developed nations) really was on non-renewable, finite resources like coal, oil, and gas. Solar energy history was made as the price of solar cells dropped dramatically to about $20 per watt.

In the 1980s through early 1990, a Los Angeles-based company called Luz Co. produced 95 percent of the world's solar-based electricity. When the price of nonrenewable fossil fuels decreased and it did not appear that federal and state government incentives would be forthcoming, investors withdrew their support and the company closed its doors. The chairman of the board said the failure of the world's largest solar electric company was not due to technological or business judgment failures, but rather to failures of government regulatory bodies to recognize the economic and environmental benefits of solar thermal generating plants.

Today there is a renewed focus and interest in solar energy as more and more people see its advantages and it becomes more affordable. World governments are offering financial assistance to companies developing and constructing solar energy systems. Such systems are now used to power many homes, businesses, holiday cottages, and even villages in Africa. Today, consumers are using solar cells to power anything from household appliances to cars. As the number of people longing for a cleaner environment grows, so does the solar industry.

One of the most important factors leading to increased use of solar energy is the fact that solar cells are becoming increasingly cost-effective as more distributors enter the market and new technologies offer more choice and new products. Some scientists and economists are wondering whether the end of the combustion age will occur in our lifetime. Cars that use new fuel cells powered by solar energy and electricity are entering the market. Screen-printed solar cells are expected to drive prices down even more. Some companies are creating roofing shingles that capture the sun's rays and convert them into electricity. Solar panels are being mounted to the sides of houses when roof space is not an option, and pools are being heated with solar energy for a fraction of the price of conventional pool heaters. All in all, solar energy is gaining wider acceptance and broader uses and applications, and that trend is expected to continue in the next several years.

The History of Wind Energy

Humankind quickly figured out how to harness the energy of the wind. Wind energy propelled boats along the Nile River as early as 5000 B.C.E. By 200 B.C.E. windmills in China were pumping water. And by the 11th century, people in the Middle East were using windmills for food production and returning merchants and crusaders carried this idea back to Europe.

European settlers brought wind technology to America in the 19th century and used windmills for pumping water for farms, ranches, and later to generate electricity in people's homes and in factories. In addition to propelling the development of the steam engine, industrialization also sparked the development of larger windmills to generate electricity. These large windmills were called wind turbines, and the earliest versions appeared in Denmark as early as 1890. By the 1940s the largest wind turbine of its day started operations on a Vermont hilltop known as Grandpa's Knob. It was rated at 1.25 megawatts in winds of about 30 miles per hour and fed electric power to the local utility network for several months during World War II.

The popularity of using wind energy has always fluctuated with the price of fossil fuels. Once fuel prices fell after World War II, people lost interest in wind turbines. But then the price of oil skyrocketed in the 1970s, and interest in wind turbines again gained ground, along with research and development. The result has been wind farms or

Best Practice

Findings of 2008 Workforce Survey Reports

In 2008, surveys were conducted by the American Public Power Association, the Geothermal Energy Association, and the Solar Industry Association to gauge the future of the energy workforce. Some of their findings were:

- A significant portion of the public power workforce would be eligible to retire during the next five to seven years.

- The positions that will experience the most retirements may also be the most difficult to replace: skilled trades, first line supervisors, senior managers, and general managers/CEO.

- The most significant challenges created will be the loss of knowledge due to retirements, finding replacements, and the lack of bench strength within organizations.

- Employment is expected to increase in the coming years as geothermal plant development and research expands.

- According to the U.S. Department of Energy, building geothermal power plants creates 11 times the number of jobs as building a comparable natural gas power plant.

- As of August 2010, the U.S. solar industry employs an estimated 93,000 solar workers, defined as those workers who spend at least 50 percent of their time supporting solar-related activities.

wind power plants, the groups of turbines that feed electricity into the utility grid, in the United States and Europe. Today Texas, Iowa, and California have the largest number of wind farms generating power. Oregon and Washington are also leading states with wind generation facilities. It is estimated, however, that only 1 percent of the energy consumed by the country is currently provided by wind generation. But that is expected to increase dramatically over the next few decades, as around 40 percent of all new generation capacity added to the electric grid in the United States in 2009 stemmed from wind power projects, according to the American Wind Energy Association.

A Political History of the Petroleum Industry

Until the early 1960s, crude oil or petroleum was produced by several countries, including the United States, Mexico, and Venezuela as well as other Persian Gulf countries. However, there was growing concern about the United States' increasing dependence on Persian Gulf oil. In 1959 the U.S. government established the Mandatory Oil Import Quota program (MOIP), which was intended to restrict the amount of oil imported into the United States by other countries and encourage the use of oil produced by the United States and other countries in North and South America such as Mexico and Venezuela.

This act by the U.S. government led to a depression in prices of Persian Gulf oil. In response to this, four Persian Gulf oil producing nations, Iran, Iraq, Kuwait, and Saudi Arabia, along with Venezuela, formed The Organization of the Petroleum Exporting Countries (OPEC) in order to coordinate and unify petroleum policies among its member countries and secure fair and stable prices for these petroleum producers. OPEC was originally located in Geneva, Switzerland, and relocated to Vienna, Austria, in 1965.

Since then, other members have joined and left OPEC: Qatar in 1961; Indonesia in 1962, which then suspended its membership in January 2009; Socialist Peoples Libyan Arab Jamahiriya in 1962; United Arab Emirates in 1967; Algeria in 1969; Nigeria in 1971; Ecuador in 1973, which suspended its membership from December 1992 to October 2007; Angola in 2007; and Gabon from 1975 to 1994.

How well OPEC has achieved its goals depends on which perspective one views it from. With oil prices continuing to soar, consumers would say it has succeeded. From some economists' viewpoint, oil prices have been impacted less by OPEC and more by increased demand in Asia, increasing competition and creating increased prices. However, there is little doubt that OPEC has had an impact on the history of petroleum in the United States.

The Mideast Oil Crisis

There has never been an event in history that affected the energy industry as powerfully as the Mideast Oil Crisis. In October, 1973, panic gripped the United States. The crude oil rich Middle-Eastern countries cut off exports of petroleum to Western nations because of their involvement in recent Arab-Israeli conflicts. Although the oil embargo would probably not have made a big impact on the United States, panicking investors and oil companies caused a gigantic surge in oil prices. The situation was caused more by fear and irrationality than any firm economic basis and turned out to be one of the most memorable of the 1970s. The Mideast Oil Crisis created long lines at the gas pump due to petroleum shortages and high gasoline prices.

The beginning of the crisis was actually after World War II, when the allied powers created a Zionist state known as Israel to serve as a homeland for the millions of disfranchised Jews throughout the world. Israel was proclaimed an independent nation by its people on May 14, 1948. The new country's land consisted of Palestine, which was previously controlled by the British. Although the Jews agreed to the settlement, local Arabs refused to acknowledge the Israeli state and attacked the new country's borders throughout the following year. The attacks eventually escalated into a full-scale conflict known as the Suez-Sinai War.

The British and the French took the part of the Israelis in order to punish Egyptian president Gomar Nasser for claiming control of the Suez Canal. A decisive action on the part of the United Nations resolved the conflict. In response to this, the Arabs united against the Israelis. An Arab attack force gathered along Israel's borders in 1967 and the Israelis launched an attack. This conflict came to be known as the Six Day War. Backed by Western countries, with the primary supporter being France, Israel succeeded in destroying the Arab forces and claimed the Gaza Strip, the Sinai Peninsula, the Golan Heights, East Jerusalem, and the West Bank from the neighboring countries of Syria, Jordan, and Egypt.

In 1973, Arab forces led by Egypt and Syria launched their own attach on Yom Kippur, the holiest of Jewish holidays. The Arabs did not succeed, but their tactics impressed the Soviet Union, and they provided the Arabs with technology to use against Israel. It was then that the Arab nations abruptly stopped exporting oil to countries such as the United States and the Netherlands. Eventually the United States helped to resolve the Israeli-Arab conflict, but its economic impact was still being felt. Panic caused inflated gas prices. Gas rationing caused long lines at gas stations.

There were more oil scares throughout the next two decades. One occurred when the Shah of Iran was deposed during a revolution in that country. During the revolution, petroleum exports decreased greatly, causing crude oil prices to once again be raised by an exorbitant amount. Further, Iraq's invasion of Kuwait in the 1990s also inflated oil prices for a short period of time. These trends have led many people worldwide to question the world's dependence on Middle Eastern oil and call for the development of new energy sources not tied to any particular geographic region of the planet.

Today's Energy Industry

Today, people have more energy source choices than ever before. Energy production takes many forms, from traditional electric generation to nuclear power, solar energy, and wind energy. Still, most energy produced in the industrialized world comes from fossil fuels: coal, natural gas, and crude oil. Fossil fuels account for 80 percent of total energy production at a value of an estimated $150 billion.

Here in the United States, residents are fortunate that the country is a treasure trove, containing vast amounts of natural energy resources. Unfortunately, the country's apparently insatiable hunger for inexpensive energy has led to what has become the status quo: its demand for energy now outpaces its energy production. Up until the 1960s and 1970s, the United States was mostly energy self-sufficient. Over the years, however, as the country's population and economy grew, so did its total energy use. From 1949 to 2000 the population in the United States increased 89 percent, from 149 million people to 281 million. During that same period, total energy consumption in the United States grew more than three times its original number, from 32 quadrillion British thermal units (Btu) to 98 quadrillion Btu.

Despite this unparalleled and rapid increase in energy consumption, researchers and conservationists have worked to improve energy efficiencies from improving furnaces, fuel efficiency, and appliances, to information campaigns to teach consumers how to reduce their energy consumption. The result us that U.S. energy efficiency has vastly improved over the years, particularly when energy use is compared to the gross domestic product (GDP). Between 1949 and 2000, the amount of energy required to generate one dollar of GDP output fell from 20,600 Btu to 10,600 Btu, an increase in efficiency of 49 percent.

No one can argue that energy drives the industrialized U.S. economy. According to the United States Energy Information Agency,

Americans spend more than half a trillion dollars a year on energy. This energy consumption can be broken down into four main categories of users: industrial, transportation, commercial, and residential. The industrial category is the largest of the four main energy consuming users, with approximately three-fifths of the energy consumed used in manufacturing, with the remainder being used by mining, construction, agriculture, and fisheries operations.

The United States Energy Information Agency predicts that worldwide energy consumption is projected to increase 50 percent by the year 2030. This also means a 50 percent increase in carbon dioxide emissions. Along with the realization of the diminishing supplies of fossil fuels, this has led to a changing—yet dynamic—period in the energy industry. Along with the challenges the industry is facing comes a renewed emphasis on pollution control, energy efficiency, and the development of clean, renewable energy sources.

As part of its effort to encourage the use of cleaner green energy sources, the United States Department of Energy (DOE) launched Open Energy Information (OpenEI.org), a new open-source Web platform that provides DOE resources and data to the public. The information found there is free, editable, and produced using an evolving wiki-platform that the DOE hopes will help to deploy clean energy technologies across the country and the world. The site provides information nationwide on programs that offer tax credits as well as opportunities to improve the environment through "green tag" purchases (items that are considered energy conserving). The incentives listed on the site can be used by all sorts of end-users, including government entities, businesses, or consumers. The Incentive Programs Gateway is an evolving source of information on financing renewable energy that the DOE hopes will increase the installation and use of these products and energy sources.

A Brief Chronology

1 million B.C.E.: Early humans learn to control fire.

5000 B.C.E.: Wind energy propels boats along the Nile River.

1000 B.C.E.: People in the Middle East use windmills for food production. Returning merchants and crusaders carry this idea back to Europe.

1200 B.C.E.: Natives of Polynesia learn how to use wind to propel their sail boats, using sails.

200 B.C.E.: Simple windmills in China pump water.

1400: Industries, in the form of large milling facilities, come to depend on water power for energy.

1770: Large water powered cotton mills are operated by William Strutt and Richard Arkwright.

1800: Steam engines join waterwheels in powering English textile mills.

1820: Large, water-powered, industrial cities are created.

1860: Solar energy is first developed by Auguste Mouchout of France.

1879: Edison's invention of the incandescent lamp makes indoor lighting possible.

1883: Charles Fritz turns the sun's rays into electricity.

1887: Nicolai Tesla, who once worked for Edison, devises an electrical theory using alternating current, which he authenticates in 30 separate patents.

1890: Wind turbines appear in Denmark.

1895: Westinghouse builds the Ames Hydroelectric Generating Plant, near Ophir, Colorado, and the original Niagara Falls Adams Power Plant.

Late 1890s: Marie Curie discovers elements that are radioactive.

1930s: Enrico Fermi produces artificial radiation by bombing uranium atoms with neutrons.

1940s: The largest wind turbine of the time begins operating on a Vermont hilltop known as Grandpa's Knob.

1942: The Manhattan Project is created.

1945: The United States drops atomic bombs on Nagasaki and Hiroshima in Japan.

1950s: The Atomic Energy Commission works with public utilities to develop electric power generation using nuclear fission.

1951: The first nuclear reactor to produce electricity is the small experimental breeder reactor (EBR-1) in Idaho, which starts up in December.

1954: Calvin Fuller, Gerald Pearson, and Daryl Chaplin of Bell Laboratories accidentally discover the use of silicon as a semiconductor, which leads to the construction of a solar panel with an efficiency rate of 6 percent.

1956: The first commercial solar cell is made available to the public at a very expensive $300 per watt.

1958: Vanguard I, the first satellite to use solar energy to generate electricity, is launched.

1960: Yankee Rowe, The first fully commercial nuclear power plant, starts up in 1960 and operates until 1992.

1973: The Mideast Oil Crisis takes place, causing oil prices to skyrocket.

1979: A partial core meltdown occurs in a nuclear reactor at the Three Mile Island nuclear power plant in Pennsylvania.

1980s: Los Angeles-based company Luz Co. produces 95 percent of the world's solar-based electricity.

1986: A meltdown at the Chernobyl nuclear power plant emits radiation.

1986: Physicists Karl Müller and Johannes Bednorz are able to achieve superconductivity in lanthanum barium copper oxide (LBCO) at a temperature of 35K.

1990: The U.S. Pollution Prevention Act of 1990 is enacted.

Late 1990s: The first of the third-generation nuclear reactors is commissioned.

2000: The population in the United States has increased to 281 million people; total energy consumption in the United States reaches 98 quadrillion Btu.

Chapter 2

State of the Industry

The energy industry has a profound effect on every person on every continent of our planet. It locates, creates, engineers, transports, advocates for, and cleans up after all of the energy sources that humans have discovered to date, from firewood and fossil fuels to wind power and nuclear energy. Populations all over the world consume large amounts of fuel, making the energy industry one of the most important players in the infrastructure and maintenance of society. The industry includes the following sectors:

→ Petroleum industry
→ Natural gas industry
→ Coal industry
→ Electrical power industry
→ Nuclear power industry
→ Renewable energy industry

Worldwide Energy Consumption

Eighty to 90 percent of worldwide energy consumption—estimated in 2008 at 474 exajoules—is derived from either the direct use of fossil fuels or the combustion of fossil fuels to generate electricity.

While energy consumption is loosely correlated with gross national product (GNP) and climate, the United States consumes a disproportionate amount of energy, even when compared to other highly developed countries. For example, the consumption rates for Japan and Germany average about 6 kilowatts (kW) per person; the United States has an average consumption rate of 11.4 kW per person. In subtropical or tropical developing countries the per person energy use is closer to 0.7 kW.

With 5 percent of the world's population and 22 percent of the global GNP, the United States consumes about 25 percent of the world's energy. China, with an energy rate of 1.6 kilowatts per person, is experiencing the most the most significant growth of energy consumption. Its per-person consumption has increased 5.5 percent per year over the past 25 years.

Worldwide, industrial users (agriculture, mining, manufacturing, and construction) consume approximately 37 percent of the total energy consumption, while personal and commercial transportation consume 20 percent. Residential heating, lighting, and appliances use 11 percent, while commercial use (lighting, heating and cooling of commercial buildings, and provision of water and sewer services) amounts to 5 percent of the total. The remaining 27 percent of the world's energy is lost in transmission and generation.

A Closer Look at Energy Consumption in the United States

It was not until the 1950s that energy consumption began to outpace domestic production in the United States. With energy self-sufficiency a thing of the past, the United States began importing energy to meet its needs. By 2009, imported energy accounted for 24 percent of all energy consumed.

Energy use per person in the United States has increased every year since 1949, with the exception of the oil crisis of the mid-1970s and early 1980s and the economic downturn of 2008 and 2009. Today, Americans consume energy at a rate per person that is 44 percent greater than it was in 1949. That said, efficiency improvements, industry shifts, and structure changes in the economy since 1970 have helped ease the country's hunger for energy.

The history of the nation's energy industry is one of large-scale change, as new forms of energy are discovered and developed. Wood served as the primary form of energy until it was surpassed by coal around 1885. Despite its tremendous and rapid expansion, coal was in turn overtaken by petroleum in the middle of the 20th century.

In the second half of the 20th century, natural gas experienced rapid development, and coal began to expand again. Late in the century, hydroelectric power and nuclear electric power were developed, and supplied significant amounts of energy.

The U.S. Energy Information Administration's *Annual Energy Outlook 2010* projects that fossil fuels will continue to provide the majority of the energy consumed in the United States in the next 25 years, assuming that current laws and regulations remain unchanged. As the use of renewable forms of energy grows, however, the fossil-fuel share of overall energy consumption is predicted to decline. For example, non-hydroelectric renewable energy is projected to double by 2035.

Non-Renewable versus Renewable Energy Sources

The key division between types of energy sources is whether they are renewable or non-renewable; that is, whether they can be reproduced naturally, or whether they are difficult to reproduce at the rate at which they are used.

Non-Renewable Energy Sources

Non-renewable resources, by definition, cannot be produced, grown, generated, or used on a scale that can sustain their rate of consumption. They are resources that are consumed much faster than nature can create them. Fossil fuels such as natural gas, oil, and coal, are prime examples of non-renewable energy sources. While fossil fuels are relatively inexpensive to harvest, they form very slowly over thousands of years. The largest non-renewable energy sectors today are the petroleum, natural gas, and coal industries.

Renewable Energy Sources

Renewable energy refers to energy generated using resources that are naturally replenished as long as they are properly conserved. Unlike fossil fuels, renewable energy sources—such as hydropower and tidal power, wind power, geothermal power, and solar power, and biomass power—cannot be depleted. Currently, renewable energy meets approximately 13 percent of the global energy demand, and 6 percent of demand for energy in the United States.

The renewable energy sector has grown significantly over the past few decades. In 2004, renewable energy supplied approximately 7 percent of the world's energy consumption. In 2005, the total new investment in renewable energy was estimated at $38 billion resulting in an additional 35 gigawatts of capacity. Along with the growth in investments and capacity is a growth in employment opportunities in renewable energy and energy efficiency programs. In 1995, more than 45,000 jobs were directly or indirectly related to energy efficiency and renewable energy programs, a number that has grown rapidly in subsequent years.

Everyone
Knows

Four Types of Power Companies

The United States electric power industry is primarily composed of four primary types of companies:

For-profit power companies generate, distribute, and sell electrical power to their residential, commercial, and governmental customers. When they are not able to meet demand for electricity, they may choose to buy power from brokers or non-utility generators.

Public utility companies are nonprofit companies that supply power to municipalities, counties, or even an entire state. They may generate the electricity, or buy it from a for-profit power company, broker, or non-utility generator.

Rural electric companies serve rural communities, providing electricity to a large geographical area, but usually a smaller number of customers.

Non-utility generators/energy brokers and marketers came into being in the late 1980s and throughout the 1990s, when deregulation meant that power companies and electric consumers could purchase their electricity through other sources than their local electric utility. These companies do not generate their own power, but buy and sell power as needed to large customers or power companies when demand is high.

The Energy Industry Workforce

The energy industry is a high tech industry; however, public perceptions do not always reflect this reality. Energy careers are often stereotyped as unstable and low-skilled. This has caused qualified workers to be unaware of the many well-paying career opportunities in the industry. The perception of many energy occupations—especially among young candidates entering the work force—is that the industry lacks clear and understandable career ladders, making it a confusing career choice.

The average age of workers in the energy industry has been on the increase over the past few decades. It is now estimated that more than 500,000 energy workers will retire within the next five to 10 years. In addition, the industry is faced with increased demand for qualified workers as new technologies are adopted, new power plants are built, and new sources of energy are explored. The industry's aging workforce, combined with the dynamic change in energy production and efficiencies, make now an ideal time to enter the energy sector workforce.

Workers enter the industry with a variety of educational backgrounds. As with any high-tech industry, the amount of education and training required correlates with the level of the position. Entry-level field jobs require little to no previous training or experience. Positions such as engineering technician require at least a two-year associate's degree in engineering technology. Upper level professional jobs such as geologist, geophysicist, or petroleum engineer, require at least a bachelor's degree, but preferably a master's degree or a Ph.D.

Issues Facing the Energy Industry

The energy sector is an industry ripe with political, social, environmental, and economical implications. Energy security, clean technologies, the expansion of nuclear power, a drive toward greater fuel efficiencies, pollution, greenhouse gas emissions, and toxic waste disposal are just a few of the issues regularly debated and discussed in the U.S. government and in the nation's media outlets. With both the wind and solar energy industries rapidly expanding, renewable energy is currently the fastest growing segment of the electric power industry, even though it remains a small piece of the nation's overall energy mix. As this technology grows and its implementation expands, companies are hiring a significant number of new workers.

The natural gas industry also is evolving and changing. The business and residential use of natural gas has reached a plateau; however, the use of the fuel has grown substantially as a clean alternative to coal in generating electricity, and even as an alternative fuel in transportation.

Energy Industry by Sector

Below find general overviews of each key sector of the energy industry.

Petroleum Industry

A fossil fuel, petroleum finds many uses worldwide. In the energy industry, its primary uses are as fuel oil and gasoline. Companies within the petroleum industry work to explore and find new sources of petroleum, extract, refine, and transport it to various customers. Nearly every country in the world relies on petroleum as fuel, gasoline for vehicles, and as a base ingredient of many industrial products. Developed countries use more petroleum than others, with the United States consuming approximately 25 percent of all the oil produced each year. Europe, Asia, and the Middle East also consume a great deal of petroleum.

According to the American Petroleum Institute, there are more than 450 oil and natural gas companies in the United States alone. This energy sector employs more than 9.2 million people and contributes 7.5 percent of the nation's economy, or $1 trillion. In the United States, petroleum companies have worked to reduce their carbon footprints. The industry has invested $58.4 billion in zero- and low-carbon emissions technologies since 2000.

Natural Gas Industry

A clear and odorless gas, natural gas is extracted from underground deposits and transported through pressurized pipelines to local distribution companies that depressurize it, add odor to it, and deliver it to industrial, residential, and commercial customers. The vast natural gas pipeline system runs 2.3 million miles, including local utility distribution mains, utility distribution pipes, and transmission lines.

According the U.S. Department of Energy, the consumption of natural gas is expected to increase by 20 percent over the next 20 years. It currently accounts for nearly 25 percent of all energy use in the United States. Much of the popularity of natural gas is due to its cleanliness, efficiency, and reliability, and most of its growth in demand is for generating electricity, where it is quickly replacing coal as the fuel of choice. In fact, due to new environmental regulations, power company executives say that new generating plants will be fueled by natural gas rather than coal.

Natural gas remains one sector of the energy industry in which the United States is relatively self-sufficient. Eighty-four percent of the natural gas consumed in the United States is produced in the United States, with Canada producing most of the rest. Vast quantities of natural gas have been discovered in the North Slope region of Alaska, but these supplies cannot be tapped until an Alaskan natural gas pipeline is built.

Another method for transporting natural gas is in the form of liquid natural gas (LNG). Natural gas is temporarily converted to liquid form so that it can be easily stored and transported to markets where is it regasified and distributed. Imports of LNG are projected to increase from 3 percent of the U.S. natural gas supply in 2003 to 22 percent in 2020. Along with this growth in imports will be a growth in the number of facilities for the production and transportation of LNG. The U.S. currently gets a majority of its LNG from Trinidad and Tobago, Qatar, Algeria, Nigeria, Oman, Australia, Indonesia, and the United Arab Emirates.

Coal Industry

Considered by environmentalists to be the most polluting fuel, and the largest source of leading greenhouse gas carbon dioxide (CO_2), coal is currently used to generate more than half of all of the electricity (52 percent) used in the United States. However, coal production has been decreasing. For the first time in more than forty years, U.S. coal production decreased for a second consecutive year. In 2000, coal production declined to 1,073.6 million short tons— 2.4 percent less than 1999. (Tons in Britain are measured at 2,240 pounds, and are called long tons; in the United States, a ton is 2,000 pounds, and is called a short ton.) Nevertheless, overall coal consumption increased in 2000. The additional needs of the industry were answered by a substantial reduction in stocks of coal by 43.4 million short tons. This reduction in production of coal stock lowered year-end stock levels by 23.7 percent from 1999 levels.

Coal prices, on an annual basis, declined in 2000, continuing the downward trend of the last several years. Although there were higher prices for some of the consuming sectors as a result of the increasing fuel costs at the end of the year (on a delivered basis, which means cost of delivery was included), the average price of utility coal (on a delivered basis) declined 1.8 percent, for an annual average of $24.28 per short ton (120.1 cents per million Btu). Coking coal prices dropped to $44.37 per short ton, a 3.2-percent decline over the 1999 price. The price of other industrial steam coal was slightly lower in 2000 with an annual average price of $31.44 per short ton.

Exports and Imports

From 1999 to 2000, total U.S. coal exports remained unchanged at 58.5 million short tons, reversing a three-year decline. The highly competitive world coal market was again dominated by Australia, the leading coal exporting country. The strong U.S. dollar in 1999 and 2000 gave an edge to other coal exporting countries when contract prices were negotiated.

The market for U.S. steam coal exports dropped somewhat in 2000. Total steam coal exports were down (by 2.6 percent) to a level of 25.7 million short tons, down from 26.3 million short tons in 1999. Canada represented the largest steam coal export market for the United States, accounting for 58.1 percent of all steam coal exports in 2000, despite the 4.1 percent drop from the 1999 level. Other major declines in steam coal exports were experienced in Mexico (one million short tons) and China (0.8 million short tons). Although total steam coal exports were down overall, Japan and the United Kingdom increased their share of U.S. steam coal exports. The increases of 38.1 percent for the United Kingdom and 28.2 percent for Japan were not enough to compensate for the declines by other countries.

Coal imports, although an extremely small part of the total U.S. coal supply (less than 1 percent of total consumption), increased dramatically in 2000. Total coal imports were 12.5 million short tons, an increase of 37.7 percent. The rise in imports in 2000 was attributable to the heightened demand for low sulfur coal to meet the stricter sulfur emission requirements of Phase II of the Clean Air Act Amendments (CAAA) of 1990.

Electric utilities accounted for 60 percent of all coal imports with other power producers accounting for approximately 20 percent. A significant portion of the increase can be attributed to higher receipts of imported coal by utilities in Alabama. The average price of U.S. coal imports for 2000 was $30.10 per short ton, only slightly less than the 1999 value of $30.77 per short ton. Colombia remained the largest supplier of U.S. coal imports with 7.6 million short tons, or 61 percent of all coal imports. Venezuela and Canada followed with 2 million short tons and 1.9 million short tons, respectively.

Stocks

Coal stocks at the end of 2000 totaled 140.1 million short tons, a drop of 43.4 million short tons. Stocks held by coal producers and distributors fell by 7.6 million short tons, a decrease of 19.2 percent. Industrial users, including coke plants, held a total of 6.1 million short tons, a decrease of 1.4 million short tons. Coal stocks in the electric power sector declined by 34.4 million short tons in 2000, helping to keep production levels down. The colder than normal weather in many parts of the country, combined with the tight coal market at the end of the year, kept inventories at levels well below historical level.

Electric Power

To generate electricity, electric plants harness high pressure steam, flowing water, or some other force of nature to spin the blades of a turbine, which is attached to an electric generator. When electricity leaves a generating plant, its voltage is stepped up to the level of the power grid. Transmission lines supported by huge towers connect generating plants with industrial customers and substations. At substations, the electricity's voltage is reduced and made available for household and small business use via distribution lines, which usually are carried by electric poles or buried underground.

Electricity is used in every home and business in the United States and is a major utility across the globe. In 2008, the United States consumed 1,379 billion kilowatt-hours of electricity, according to the U.S. Department of Energy. The electric power industry is highly regulated by the U.S. government, despite much of the deregulation efforts of the previous decades. Today, the U.S. government still defines standards and guidelines for the industry, dictating issues such as reliability, and rates charged to consumers.

The Smart Grid
The Smart Grid refers to modernizing the national electrical transmission and distribution system. Nationwide "Smart Grid initiatives" have several goals, including increasing reliability of the delivery of electricity, allowing more generation sources to supply electricity from more diverse locations, and allowing for improved monitoring and management of the use of electricity. Some aspects that could be considered part of a Smart Grid initiative include:

- **Smart meters:** An electric meter installed in the user's facility that tracks how much energy the consumer is using and when the energy is being consumed.
- **Substation automation:** A reliable, self-healing power system that responds quickly to real time events that occur at a substation, such as lightning strikes, with appropriate actions, like bringing other energy sources online, to ensure uninterrupted power services to the end-users it serves.
- **Load balancing:** Some Smart Grid technology can monitor the energy loads of various electric systems so that the load can be better balanced between systems.
- **Demand response:** Smart Grid technology is looking to actually turn off or decrease generation of electricity when demand is lower, and bring online generating capacity when the demand increases.
- **Transmission planning:** Like it sounds, energy distributors look at long-term trends in energy to ensure transmission of energy is available as needed throughout a system.

Non-Utility Generators
Due to the deregulation of the utility industry that occurred in the 1990s, new companies have developed to generate electricity to sell directly to large manufacturing clients, government utility companies, and other for-profit utility companies. Called non-utility generators, these companies generate power and sell it to others that need it, without the added expense of maintaining and repairing distribution lines. Often their power is transmitted using the same transmission lines as other utilities, and distributed using other

companies' distribution lines, for which they pay a maintenance fee. However, they are able to offer their customers cheaper power because of their reduced costs.

Nuclear Power

Prior to the earthquake in Japan that occurred on March 11, 2011, there had been a resurgence in the interest in nuclear power, thanks to the concern over the world's dependence on fossil fuels and their associated effects on the environment. In addition to increased interest, there had been a corresponding increase in use. For example, in 2006, 16 percent of the world's total electricity production came from nuclear sources. In 2010, that percentage rose to 25 percent. In the United States, nuclear energy accounts for about 20 percent of all energy produced in the country. Worldwide, there are 440 nuclear reactors in operation.

General approval of the use of nuclear energy was verified in a Zogby Interactive poll that showed that two-thirds of Americans, or 67 percent, supported the construction of new nuclear power plants in the United States, with 46 percent showing strong support for new nuclear plants. This survey echoed a trend reported in the 2007 Saint Index (a survey that indicates if there are objections to specific

Fast
Facts

Where Are the Jobs?

Here are some of the latest statistics about the number of jobs in the major energy industry sectors:

- The oil and natural gas industry supports more than 9.2 million jobs in the United States.
- The total number of jobs supported by the existing geothermal industry is 18,000.
- The U.S. solar industry employs an estimated 93,000 solar workers.
- Electric power generation, transmission, and distribution provided about 404,700 jobs in the United States.

land uses, and who is objecting to them) showing that the number of Americans supporting power plant development in their hometowns rose dramatically. Thirty-eight percent of American adults supported a local power plant project, compared to just 23 percent in 2006.

Political support was also evident. Republicans, at 85 percent, and unaffiliated voters, at 70 percent, were more likely than Democrats (49 percent) to support the construction of new nuclear power plants. A majority of respondents of all ages expressed support for building new nuclear power plants, with the greatest overall support among those age 65 and older (78 percent).

In comparison, a relatively high number of Americans (71 percent) support building new natural gas power plants in the United States, while 51 percent support the construction of new coal power plants, and 38 percent support construction of new oil power plants. Smaller percentages support the construction of new natural gas (34 percent), coal (27 percent), or oil (19 percent) power plants. Saint Index results also showed that most people supported federal government financial support of nuclear (28 percent), solar (18 percent), and wind (12 percent) fuel sources. Just 8 percent believe most of the federal government's financial support should be focused on biomass, while 4 percent each favored geothermal, hydro, oil, coal, or natural gas.

All of this support and increased interest and use was good news for the nuclear industry and its potential employees. More than 20 nuclear facilities were in the planning stages, and adding those to the existing plants in the United States, there was every reason to expect that the number of jobs would increase, along with the number of opportunities for promotion.

The devastating earthquake and the tsunami that followed it that hit Japan on March 11, 2011, dramatically changed the future of the nuclear energy industry. The 8.9 magnitude earthquake and the subsequent tsunami destroyed the city of Sendai and impacted most of the cities along the east coast of Honshu. The earthquake also caused the cooling systems to fail at the Fukushima Nuclear Power Plant, resulting in a nuclear emergency being declared.

This disaster has once again caused concern about the safety of nuclear power plants. In the United States, concerns about battery power backups were voiced to the Nuclear Regulatory Commission. Most plants have enough energy in battery backups to last four to eight hours. But it is the prolonged lack of power (greater than eight hours) at the Fukushima plant that caused the cooling systems to fail and the subsequent concern of a nuclear meltdown.

Just days after the earthquake, U.S. Senator Joseph Lieberman suggested that the United States needs to stop the development of new nuclear power plants until what happened at Fukushima is fully understood. Other countries are also considering measures to stop production of nuclear power plants. For example, Italy announced its one-year moratorium on the construction of nuclear power plants.

It is clear that the nuclear energy industry has been impacted by this disaster. What effects this will have on future jobs is unclear, but it is certain that the number of jobs will be impacted.

Hydropower

Hydropower is energy extracted from moving water. Essentially, it is a process of trapping the sun's energy, since the sun drives the flow of water on the planet, resulting in the hydrologic cycle. This cycle begins when the sun heats water in oceans and seas and water vapor evaporates into the air. (Ice and snow can transform directly into water vapor.) The sun also causes evapotranspiration, the process in which water transpires from plants and evaporates from the soil as it is heated.

Rising air currents carry vapor into the atmosphere, where cooler temperatures condense it into clouds. Air currents then transport water vapor around the globe as cloud particles collide, grow, and fall out of the sky as precipitation. Precipitation may fall as snow or hail, accumulating into ice caps and glaciers. However, most precipitation falls into the oceans or onto land as rain, producing runoff, which enters rivers moving toward the oceans. Runoff can also be stored in groundwater and in freshwater lakes, or it may infiltrate deep into the ground and replenish aquifers (systems for storing and distributing groundwater). All of this water eventually returns to the ocean, where the water cycle begins.

Centuries ago, Greeks used falling water to power grinding wheels. In the 18th century, it was used extensively to power mills and pumps of the industrial revolution. Today, power is produced using falling water to power electrical turbines. To mitigate the unpredictability of precipitation, water is stored behind dams to better control the availability of electricity. Among renewable sources of electricity, water is the second greatest source, with hydroelectric plants operating where suitable waterways are available.

The main advantage of hydroelectric power is that water is a source of cheap power and requires no imported fuel. Also, because there is no fuel combustion, there is little air pollution in comparison with fossil fuel plants, and limited thermal pollution compared with nuclear plants. However, the building of dams floods land and reduces a river's flow downstream, negatively impacting the habitats of local plant, fish, and animal life. As a result, the use of hydro-electric power has many opponents. The general consensus appears to be that hydropower will not grow as rapidly as other renewable energy sources due to the concerns over its environmental impacts.

Canada, Brazil, China, the United States, and Russia were the five greatest producers of hydroelectric power in 2001, accounting for 48 percent of the world's total. The U.S. Department of Energy (AEA 2004) projects no growth in hydroelectric power generation within the United States, but rather a steady state at 309,000 gigawatt-hours (gWh) compared to its peak of 354 gWh in 1997 and 308 gWh in 2003.

More than 60 percent of the worldwide increase in primary energy demand, between 2000 and 2030, will come from develop-ing countries, especially in Asia. More than a quarter of the world's population has no access to electricity and, although the number of people without power supplies will fall in the coming decades, a projected 1.4 billion people will still be without electricity in 2030. Renewable energy will play a growing role in the world's primary energy mix, and since hydropower has long been a major source of electricity production, its share in global primary energy will hold steady, but its share of electricity generation will fall.

The trend in both Canada and the United States has been to micro hydro because it has negligible environmental impacts and opens up many more locations for power generation. Micro hydro is a term used to describe much smaller hydroelectric power installations that typi-cally produce up to 100 kW of power. Micro hydro systems may be installed for a single home or a small community and are sometimes connected to electric power networks. In British Columbia alone the estimates are that micro hydro will be able to more than double elec-tricity production in the province. These installations can be found around the world, particularly in developing nations where they pro-vide an economical source of energy without the purchase of fuel.

During the winter months, the sky can be cloud covered most of the month, and solar energy systems are not able to generate enough power. During these months, micro hydro systems can be installed to complement photovoltaic solar energy systems. Water flow is not affected by the lack of sun during the winter, and in fact can be higher because of snowfalls and increased rainfall. The two sys-tems then become complementary. The micro hydro system usually consists of a water turbine and flowing water. Water typically falls from a higher elevation, and usually the higher the elevation, the higher the head, or water pressure. The other main element of a micro hydro system is flow. Generally, the most economical systems are those that do not rely on a dam and reservoir, but use a consistent, low flow of water to create energy.

The system needs to have some kind of filtering system (such as a screen) to prevent fish and debris from entering before the water travels through a power canal or a pipe to the turbine. If the water source and turbine are located at some distance from each other, the most costly part of the construction of the system will be the penstock (intake valve or structure). The turbine then converts the flow and pressure of the water to mechanical energy, and the water emerging from the turbine returns to the natural watercourse along through a channel constructed for that purpose.

Biomass and Biofuels

Bioenergy is energy extracted from biomass, which includes any plant derived of organic matter and available on a renewable basis, including dedicated energy crops and trees, agricultural food and feed crops, agricultural crop wastes and residues, wood wastes and residues, aquatic plants, animal wastes, municipal wastes, and other waste materials. Traditionally, conventional biomass comes from three distinct sources: wood, waste, and alcohol fuels.

Wood is the largest source of bioenergy, and has provided heat for thousands of years from the direct use of harvested wood, and from wood waste streams such as pulping liquor, or "black liquor," a waste product from processes of the pulp, paper, and paperboard industry. Waste is the second largest source of biomass energy, derived from municipal solid waste (MSW), manufacturing waste, or landfill gas. Additionally, biomass alcohol fuel, or ethanol, derived almost exclusively from corn, is used to oxygenate gasoline.

Biomass is potentially the world's largest and most sustainable energy source; however, the biomass energy industry cannot fulfill this potential unless it resolves the issues of sustainable management and delivery of energy to those who need it. Even though residues are currently the main sources of bioenergy, dedicated energy forestry/crops may play an increasing role in the long term. These bioenergy resources are replenished through the cultivation of energy crops, such as fast growing trees and grasses called bioenergy feedstocks.

Biorefineries, producing solid, gaseous, and liquid fuels and chemicals may be the wave of the future, along with biomass feedstocks created from energy crops that are genetically modified and grown on marginal/surplus farmland. The stated goal in the United States is to triple the use of bioenergy and bio-based products by 2010, while the long term goal of the European Union is to supply 20 percent of current primary energy supply with bio-based products. Japan is also looking for a significant increase in the use of biomass energy.

Jobs

Job creation in the biomass/biofuel energy industries stems from the areas of research and manufacturing, as well as services such as installation and distribution, sales, consulting, research, engineering, and maintenance. The European Union predicts that 515,000 new jobs will result from biomass fuel production by 2020, in part because renewable energy technologies are more labor intensive than conventional technologies for the same energy output. Likewise, in Brazil more than 700,000 rural jobs have been created in the sugar-alcohol industry.

Biomass technologies may also have a major impact on creating jobs and improving local economies in rural America. The National Energy Policy supports an increased role for biomass technologies as a new source of income for farmers, landowners, and others who harness biomass resources. To date, more than 66,000 rural jobs have been created in the production of 75 gigawatts (gW) of biopower and more than 40,000 jobs in biofuels.

According to the National Renewable Energy Laboratory, 4.9 jobs are created for every megawatt of biomass power produced, while the U.S. Department of Agriculture predicts that 17,000 jobs will be created per every million gallons of ethanol produced. The U.S. Department of Energy also estimates that advanced technologies currently under development will help the biomass power industry install more than 13,000 megawatts of biomass power by the year 2010, creating an additional 100,000 jobs.

Wind Power

The use of wind to create power is increasing worldwide. Power is created through the construction and harnessing of very large wind turbines. The World Wind Energy Association reports that the installed capacity of wind power totaled 121gW by the end of 2008, an increase of 29 percent in one year; half of this increase was in the United States, Spain, and China. Total capacity actually doubled over the preceding three years.

The growing interest in wind energy system operations is due to the fact that they do not generate air or water emissions; they do not produce hazardous waste; they do not deplete natural resources such as coal, oil, or gas; they do not cause environmental damage through resource extraction and transportation; and they do not require significant amounts of water during operation. This relatively pollution-free electricity may help reduce the environmental damage caused by power generation in the United States and worldwide.

The benefits of adopting and utilizing wind energy are far reaching and dramatic. Environmentalists predict that if energy professionals were able to develop just 10 percent of the potential wind energy available in 10 of the windiest states in the country, it would have huge impacts on the environment. One of these impacts is the ability to eradicate emissions from power plants that are fueled by coal, as well as eliminate a major source of acid rain. Another major impact is the dramatic reduction of CO_2 emissions by nearly a third. The result of these impacts on human health is also great; environmentalists say the reduced air pollution may decrease the incidences of lung conditions and diseases such as asthma. Supporters of wind energy claim that it would take development of just more than 5 percent of windy areas in the U.S. mainland to supply more than enough energy to meet current demands.

The American Wind Energy Association says that at last estimate, wind plants in the United States in 2006 generated 24 billion kilowatt-hours (kWh). When a utility company using traditional generation methods (coal-fueled generating plants) generates the same amount of energy, the result is a great deal of pollution: 30 billion pounds (15 million tons) of carbon dioxide, 76,000 tons of sulfur dioxide (208 tons per day), and 36,000 tons of nitrogen oxides (100 tons per day). While design, construction, and installation of wind turbines will cause a certain amount of emissions of these same gases, the use of the wind turbines can offset these emissions after a few months. Another factor in wind energy's favor is the fact that there is no resulting pollution when the wind turbine farms are taken down at the end of service.

It is worth noting that wind energy is a converted form of solar energy. The sun's radiation heating different parts of the Earth at different rates (day versus night, land versus water) causes absorption and reflection at different rates. As portions of the atmosphere warm differently, hot air rises, reducing the atmospheric pressure at the Earth's surface, and cooler air is drawn in to replace it, creating wind. Since air contains mass, its motion contains the energy of that motion (kinetic energy). Some portion of that energy can convert into mechanical force or electricity that we use to perform work. However, electricity currently created by wind is more costly, making it hard for power companies to justify using it. This will be one challenge that the wind energy sector will need to overcome if it is to become a bigger player in the energy industry in the future.

Solar Power

As recently as 2007, solar power connected to current electricity generating grids was considered the fastest growing source of energy. In 2009, installations of new photovoltaic generating systems increased by 83 percent, and solar energy capacity reached 15 gW. This tremendous growth is not due to usage in the United States. Germany accounts for nearly half of the increase, and Japan follows closely. In general, worldwide solar energy production has doubled every two years. This growth creates new jobs, and because the technology is fairly young and has yet to attain economies of scale, it has created more jobs per dollar invested or megawatt installed than traditional energy sources. However, since the solar industry is still fragmented, with many small companies complementing the larger original equipment manufacturers (OEMs), one has to settle for approximate employment figures. The U.S. solar electric industry employed 20,000 people directly in the year 1999, and a further 150,000 indirectly in industries such as glass and steel manufacture, electrical and plumbing contracting, architecture and system design, and battery and electrical equipment manufacture. The European solar thermal industry employed more than 10,000 in 1997 in the design, manufacture, marketing, installation, and maintenance of systems. Industry estimates indicate continued strong growth in solar energy jobs worldwide, with most new jobs in the marketing and installation of solar photovoltaic and thermal systems. The Solar Foundation published the results of its 2010 job census, which shows that there are now more than 93,000 jobs in the solar industry.

Geothermal Energy

Geothermal energy is enjoying worldwide adoption; it is currently in use in more than 70 countries. Since the beginning of the new century, geothermal energy use has increased, and by 2007, the world's geothermal energy production was 10 gW for electricity and 28 gW for heating.

Geothermal energy technologies rely on tapping the heat within the Earth itself. In the 1980s it was demonstrated that there is no equilibrium between the radiogenic heat generated in the Earth's interior and the heat dissipated into space from the Earth, which means our planet is slowly cooling down—very slowly, at less than a 350°C drop in the core temperature of about 4,000°C in 3 billion years. Therefore, geothermal energy technologies may not be technically renewable, but they do harness energy that is otherwise uselessly dissipated, and the effect on the Earth's temperature is so infinitesimal that it can realistically be regarded as renewable.

Geothermal resources range from shallow ground, to hot water and rock several miles below the Earth's surface, to the extremely high temperatures of molten rock or magma further below. This energy can be put to different uses depending upon on the temperature of the fluid extracted.

Heat Pumps versus Direct Use

Geothermal heat pumps use a system of buried pipes to transfer heat from underground to a heat exchanger at the surface, then through ductwork into buildings. The Earth's surface has an almost constant temperature of 50°F to 60.8°F. In winter, the warmer underground transfers heat to the surface, and in summer buildings at the surface transfer heat into the ground or use it to heat water. Heating and air conditioning are accomplished with one system.

Direct use relies upon access to naturally occurring hot water, which is most common in the earthquake zones of the Pacific's "Ring of Fire"; this includes the Western United States, as well as Alaska and Hawaii. Hot water is used directly to heat residential, commercial, and agricultural buildings, and to assist in processes such as fish farming and vegetable dehydration. Deep wells of a mile or more tap reservoirs of steam or very hot water used to drive turbines, which power electricity generators.

Types of Geothermal Power Plants
There are three major types of geothermal power plants.

→ **Dry steam plants**, which use geothermal steam directly, use very hot (greater than 455°F/235°C) steam and little water from a geothermal reservoir. The steam flows through a pipe to a turbine, which spins a generator and produces electricity. This type of geothermal power plant is the oldest, used first at Lardarello, Italy, in 1904.

→ **Flash steam plants** pump hot water (greater than 360°F/182°C) from a geothermal reservoir to a generator, resulting in a sudden drop in pressure that causes some water to vaporize into steam, which spins a turbine to generate electricity. Dry steam and flash steam power plants emit small amounts of carbon dioxide, nitric oxide, and sulfur, in amounts 50 times less than traditional fossil-fuel power plants. Hot water not flashed into steam is returned to the geothermal reservoir through injection wells.

→ **Binary cycle plants** developed most recently, and most new plants being built today use this technology. The water in the geothermal reservoir is forced to flow past a fluid that has a low boiling point. This causes the water in the reservoir to become vapor, and the vapor turns the turbine, which in turn generates the electricity. A Kalina geothermal system is one that uses industrial waste steam as a geothermal source. This improves the plant efficiency.

Jobs
In 1996, the U.S. geothermal energy industry as a whole provided approximately 12,300 direct jobs in the United States, and an additional 27,700 indirect jobs. The electric generation sector of the industry employed approximately 10,000 people to install and operate geothermal power plants in the United States and abroad, including power plant construction and related activities such as exploration and drilling; indirect employment was approximately 20,000 jobs. Like other renewable energy industries, the geothermal industry is said to provide more jobs per mW of energy production than conventional power production.

It appears there has been a slight decline in the number of geothermal industry jobs in the United States since 1996. The Geothermal Energy Association estimated that the geothermal industry employed about 18,000 people in 2008. This is roughly 5,000 direct jobs in operating, construction, and manufacturing and an additional 13,000 supporting jobs. Although employment is expected to increase in the coming years as geothermal plant development and research expands.

The Future

One of the most important economic aspects of geothermal energy is that it is generated with indigenous resources, reducing a nation's dependence on imported energy, and reducing trade deficits. Reducing trade deficits keeps wealth at home and promotes healthier economies. Nearly half of the U.S. annual trade deficit would be erased if imported oil were displaced with domestic energy resources.

Nearly half of all developing countries have rich geothermal resources, which could prove to be an important source of power and revenue. Geothermal projects can reduce the economic pressure of fuel imports and can offer local infrastructure development and employment. For example, one country that has installed a high amount of geothermal capacity and power generation to reduce its dependence on imported oil is the Philippines. In fact, due to this effort to increase geothermal capacity, it now offers the second largest geothermal capacity in the world, with the greatest capacity being generated by the United States. This is just one example of what is expected to become a growing trend: a developing country increasing its energy generation through renewable sources, in order to decrease dependency on fossil fuels.

Hydrogen

Hydrogen is the most plentiful element on Earth and in the universe, accounting for 90 percent of the universe by weight. It is not commonly found in its pure form, however, since it readily combines with other elements. It usually combines with oxygen in water, and in organic matter including living plants, petroleum, coal, natural gas, and other hydrocarbon compounds.

One of hydrogen's major assets is that it can be used in modified existing equipment such as reciprocating engines, turbines, and boilers with significant improvement in emissions performance; the fuel contains no carbon, therefore its combustion results in no

On the Cutting Edge

Smart Grid Technology

Electric utility companies across the country are incorporating Smart Grid technologies to their transmission and distribution systems. Smart Grid is technology that connects the generation, transmission, and distribution of electric power all the way through to each customer's meter. This system will allow the utility company to monitor, analyze, control, and communicate capabilities to the national electrical delivery system to maximize the throughput of the system while reducing energy consumption. This will allow utility companies to move power where it is needed throughout their delivery base in a more efficient and economical way. Smart Grid proponents say it will also allow end-users to use electricity more economically.

carbon monoxide or carbon dioxide, although it can result in some nitrogen oxides under certain conditions.

Before hydrogen can be used as fuel on a global scale, however, engineers and scientists must establish cost-effective processes for producing large volumes of the gas cleanly. Currently, hydrogen is prepared by electrolysis or high temperature reforming of coal or hydrocarbons. Many of the processes can create substantial pollution. For hydrogen to be pollution free, the means of preparation must also be pollution free. Scientists must also discover ways to store and distribute the gas safely. Hydrogen is the lightest element, and its low density complicates the storage and distribution issue, as does its wide explosive range and extremely low ignition energy. Hydrogen has a high-energy content per weight (nearly three times as much as gasoline), but its energy density is low under atmospheric conditions. According to Greenjobs.com, "The volumetric energy density can be increased by storing the hydrogen under elevated pressure, or storing it at extremely low temperatures as a liquid (it can also be adsorbed into metal hydrides). Hydrogen is highly flammable; it only takes a small amount of energy to ignite it. It also has a wide flammability range, meaning it can burn when its concentration in air is between 4 and 74 percent by volume."

Hydrogen's assets are also mitigated by the costs of production and distribution. Most hydrogen produced today is consumed on site, as in oil refineries, and not sold on the market. For this large-scale production, the cost is approximately $0.32 per pound when the fuel is consumed on site. When sold on the market, however, the cost of liquefying hydrogen and transporting it to the user is added to the cost of production. This can increase the selling price to $1.00 to 1.40 per pound for delivered liquid hydrogen. The ultimate goal, then, is to produce cost-effective hydrogen from renewable energy sources and make it readily available for widespread use.

Fuel Cells

The cleanest way to utilize hydrogen and oxygen to produce power is through the use of fuel cells. Sir William Grove first demonstrated fuel cell technology more than 150 years ago, in 1839. Grove used porous platinum electrodes and sulfuric acid as an electrolyte bath. William White Jaques later substituted phosphoric acid in the electrolyte bath and coined the term "fuel cell." Significant fuel cell research in Germany in the 1920s laid the groundwork for subsequent development of carbonate cycle and solid oxide fuel cells. NASA has also been using alkaline fuel cells to provide onboard electrical power for spacecraft since the 1960s.

Most fuel cells that have been derived in recent years have used hydrogen as a fuel source. These fuel cells are highly efficient and are attractive alternatives to traditional fuels because they produce very little noise or air pollution. The fuel cells take the fuel source and convert it into electricity or heat. Many of these cells produce a by-product, which is usually water.

Employment

The number of jobs in the U.S. fuel cell industry in 2002 was estimated at 4,500 to 5,500, according to Fuel Cells 2000, an independent organization dedicated to providing information about fuel cells to the public. All of the employment information included in this section was provided by this organization, which can be located online at Fuelcells.org. Here their recent analysis of jobs in the fuel cell industry:

- A few hundred jobs in venture- or angel-funded groups, primarily in research and development. Nearly three quarters of these were in the stationary sector, with the remainder in the portable sector.

- At least 500 jobs in other independent private companies, funded primarily by strategic players, distributed fairly equally between transportation, and portable and stationary sectors.
- Two thousand jobs in public "pure play" fuel cell companies, divided fairly equally between the stationary and transportation sectors.
- Internal employment by major strategic players in the U.S. fuel cell industry is estimated at roughly 1,500 to 2,000 at present, divided equally between the transportation and stationary sectors.
- Fuel cell component manufacturers appear to employ roughly 400 to 500 people in the areas of development of MEAs and membranes, and bi-polar plates.

The Future of the Energy Industry

About half of the 400,000 power industry workers in the United States are eligible to retire in the next five to 10 years, according to Carnegie Mellon University's Electricity Industry Center. Baby boomer retirements are projected to open up opportunities for qualified entrants into the energy industry. However, there may not be enough young power industry workers in the pipeline to fill these vacancies, and the nation may face a shortage of utility workers just as it gears up for the biggest wave of construction in decades to meet soaring power demand.

The crunch is already affecting cities, slowing new hookups for electric service, delaying post-storm power restorations, and forcing utilities to skimp on maintenance. The shortage exists across job categories, from line workers and plant operators to senior engineers. "It's creating a real serious crisis," says Michael Brown, a consultant for Hay Group's national energy practice. "Everything in this country runs on electricity."

Exacerbating this is the fact that the industry has trimmed about 40 percent of its workforce since 1990 in response to deregulation. During the 1990s, many states froze electric rates and utilities cut payrolls to fatten profits and offset losses from the low priced sale of power plants. Companies also shut down or scaled back training programs. These actions undercut the main appeal of a utility job: stable, lifelong employment. Today, high school graduates "are looking at jobs with computers sitting in an office, rather than working with their hands," says Jim Hunter, utility director for the International Brotherhood of Electrical Workers (IBEW) union. These graduates may not realize that a line worker is among the country's highest-paid jobs that do not require a college degree. Average annual salaries, with overtime, are $75,000. Most line workers today make more than $100,000 per year.

One drawback of working in the electricity industry, however, is the potential danger: line workers handle wires bristling with up to 765,000 volts of electricity, and electric shocks and fires each year injure or kill dozens of line workers who are not adequately protected. Positions as operations managers and engineers are less hazardous, but may also lack popularity. Most technically-minded college graduates are opting for careers in the areas of software development, aerospace, and biotech industries instead of power engineering. Today, college bachelor degree programs turn out about 500 power engineering grads a year, compared to nearly 2,000 in the 1980s, says Dennis Ray of the Power Systems Engineering Research Center.

This is a problem, since power demand is projected to soar by 50 percent by the year 2030, and utilities are planning hundreds of plants and thousands of miles of transmission lines to meet this demand. Especially affected is the nuclear power industry, which is girding for a revival after a decades-long construction hiatus following the 1979 Three Mile Island partial meltdown. The 33 nuclear reactors on the drawing board "will not get built as quickly as we want," says Dale Klein, chairman of the Nuclear Regulatory Commission. "You will see regions where there are shortages of electricity" that may trigger blackouts or brownouts.

In response to the shortage, companies like Bonneville Power Administration in the Pacific Northwest are scrambling to fill the shortfall by offering hiring bonuses of up to 25 percent of annual salary to skilled workers. First Energy in Ohio also hired 1,000 workers each of the past two years, and plans to continue that pace through 2015, doubling its workforce, says spokeswoman Ellen Raines.

The industry is also fanning out to sell students and guidance counselors on a career in the power industry, and Gulf Power in northern Florida has started a power industry academy at two local high schools. Companies such as American Electric Power and First Energy are setting up courses for skilled workers at community colleges, often paying students' tuition. Such two-year programs can significantly shorten a line worker's typical five-year apprenticeship. Meanwhile,

INTERVIEW

The Cutting Edge—Conservation

Donald Gilligan
President, National Association of Energy Service Companies (NAESCO),
Washington, D.C.

When it comes to jobs in the industry, where are you seeing the most growth, and why?
Today we are seeing the most growth coming from public sectors such as the federal, state, and local governments, in terms of sheer dollar growth. Commercial building clients are also growing, but the dollars are not has high as the public sector.

What characteristics should someone have to succeed in the industry?
If you look at energy efficiency, this is the most sophisticated part of the business. It takes very skilled sales people with a track record of selling complicated deals. It can take 12 to 24 months to develop these complex, multimillion dollar deals. You have to have a lot of experience, although

Exelon, General Electric, and others are providing research grants and scholarships for power engineering programs at four-year colleges.

Production workers in the utilities industry had average weekly earnings of $1,231 in 2008. Earnings varied by industry segment within utilities. Wages for production workers were higher on average in natural gas distribution and in electric power generation than in water, sewage, and other systems.

Government Regulation

With energy and fuel being so vitally important to the United States, it is not surprising that the U.S. government has sought to regulate it. No facet or segment of the industry has escaped government regulation, including electric generation and distribution, petroleum, coal, and natural gas sectors. Not only does the government regulate many aspects of these industries, but in recent years they have also instituted regulations to lessen the impact of their use on the environment.

that depends on the company. There are some that will hire inexperi-enced people if they have a strong background in energy engineering.

There is also a demand for energy engineers. Colleges and universi-ties didn't have programs specifically for energy engineers in the past, but that is changing. There is demand for these jobs with service com-panies, utility companies, and consulting firms. If you are an engineer that can also talk and write well, that is quite valuable.

The third type of job that is in demand is general manager, al-though that position is usually recruited inside the business. The typical career path is you start out on the engineering side or the sales side, distinguishing yourself. Then you are promoted to sales manager. Depending on the company, the sales manager may be located at the company headquarters or in a branch office. Typically if you prove to be a good manager of others you are promoted as a manager. If you're really good in sales, you stay in sales.

What is your advice to people who would like to launch a career in the energy service industry?
I would suggest starting out as an energy engineer. That is the most typical path, and there is a natural progression in the business. If you have a distinguished career in sales, selling multimillion dollar deals, you will be recognized and promoted.

These environmental regulations have and will continue to have a huge impact on energy companies and how they do business.

Regulation of Power Companies

There are two main regulatory agencies for power companies. Each state has its own Public Utilities Commission (PUC), which oversees the utility companies of the state, and the Federal Energy Regu-latory Commission (FERC) regulates the interstate transmission of natural gas, oil, and electricity. FERC also regulates natural gas and hydropower projects. In some states, the PUC also regulates tele-phone companies, rail companies, natural gas companies, and water and wastewater companies.

The PUC of each state works with each utility company under its jurisdiction to ensure that consumers are receiving power and being treated fairly. The PUC can dictate most aspects of how the utility operates, from how it sets its rates, to how it collects money from past due customers. It can also serve as an intermediary when the consumer has a complaint against the utility company.

FERC, on the other hand, regulates the transmission and wholesale sales of electricity in interstate commerce, the transmission and sale of natural gas for resale in interstate commerce, protects the reliability of the high voltage interstate transmission system through mandatory reliability standards, and monitors and investigates energy markets, among other things. All of this means that the utility company must refer to PUC and FERC guidelines and requirements as it develops and implements all operational procedures and policies. In some cases it also has to apply to the PUC for approval when it seeks to raise its rates. It must be able to justify the rate hike.

Regulation of the Petroleum Sector

Regulation of the petroleum/oil industry began in the 1970s as a result of the Organization of Petroleum-Exporting Countries (OPEC) oil embargo during those years. These countries withheld the export of oil in objection of the United States' support of Israel. At the same time, the United States was decreasing its own production of petroleum. Since this time, the U.S. government has worked to decrease the country's dependence on foreign oil by developing its own sources of energy and producing its own oil through offshore drilling exploration.

Today, government regulation is concerned with the safe exploration and production of oil, rather than regulating the business or pricing itself. This means accomplishing these without any negative impacts to the environment and surrounding wildlife. Given the 2010 disaster in the Gulf of Mexico, greater environmental regulation continues to be called for, and U.S. citizens are calling for more oversight.

Regulation of the Coal Sector

Over the years, the coal industry has been regulated for a variety of reasons. The primary struggle has been with high-cost coal producers and low-cost coal producers. A great deal of the nation's coal is produced in underground mine in the region of the country called Appalachia, in the mountains of Kentucky, West Virginia, and Virginia. Employees of these mines are unionized, which helped to protect their safety and ensure they were paid a reasonable wage for the dangerous work they performed. However, it made the price of the coal they produced much more expensive than coal produced at non-unionized mines or at surface mines. The high-cost producers called upon regulators to even the playing field by mandating that mines incorporate stringent safety and health regulations in 1969.

In the next decade, however, most surface mines were also unionized, which led to more equitable coal pricing. Because of this, the call for regulation subsided. Today, like the petroleum industry, most government regulation focuses on the environmental impacts of coal mining and its use, rather than its business operations and pricing. The coal industry has been greatly impacted by some provisions of the Clean Air Act. The Clean Air Act classifies a total of 200 substances as hazardous air pollutants (HAPs); 11 of these occur in small amounts in coal. Industrial companies that generate these substances or emit them in high enough quantities are required to use technology to reduce their emission. Many electric power-generating plants burn coal to produce energy, and they are now looking to use natural gas and other fuel sources in future plants rather than using coal. In the meantime, some utilities are consuming coal with sulfur contents substantially below the regulated levels.

Regulation of the Natural Gas Sector

As already mentioned, today the transmission and sale of natural gas for resale in interstate commerce is regulated by the Federal Energy Regulatory Commission. Under the Eisenhower presidency, government regulation of natural gas prices led to market distortions. Artificially low prices led to a decrease in natural gas production and eventual shortages of natural gas in the 1970s. It was not until the U.S. government phased out all price regulations, deregulating that segment of the industry in 1989 that the natural gas industry was able to adjust and develop a true supply and demand pricing structure. Today the FERC focuses primarily on the safe interstate transport of natural gas. In 1992, the FERC ordered gas transmission companies to unbundle their products so that suppliers and consumers would have more choices of where to purchase their natural gas.

Environmental Regulations

Today, all sectors of the energy industry are impacted by the U.S. government's environmental regulations. These regulations began in 1975 with the Energy Policy and Conservation Act of 1975. This act was a response to OPEC's embargo. It created the Strategic Petroleum Reserve to counter any severe disruptions in the country's petroleum supply, and it also created corporate average fuel economy (CAFE) standards for automobile manufacturers. At this time, manufacturers were required to double the fuel efficiency in the cars they produced to 27.5 miles per gallon by 1985. The goal of this act is to reduce the country's consumption of petroleum.

Another key piece of government regulation that has impacted the energy industry is the Clean Air Act and its revisions. The original Clean Air Act was passed in 1970 and its goal was to prevent and reduce air pollution and improve air quality in the country. Corporations were required to reduce emissions of pollutants that were defined by the Environmental Protection Agency. In 1990, revisions to the Clean Air Act were enacted and designed to reduce acid rain and other environmental hazards. The Clean Air Act has had a direct impact on the coal industry and the electric power industries, since many of them burn coal to generate power. Power companies are now looking for alternative fuel sources to generate power. In the meantime, using additional technology to reduce pollutants has created additional costs and impacted the price of energy.

The Energy Policy Act of 1992 is important because it introduced a key driver of the renewable energy industry, the production tax credit (PTC). The PTC offers a subsidy of 1.5 cents per kilowatt-hour generated to independent power producers (companies that generate power without transmitting it to end-users; instead they resell it to utility companies and large customers; also known as non-utility generators). This subsidy continues for a period of 10 years from the beginning of power generation. Because energy generation from renewable sources can be more costly, this subsidy spurred the development and investment of renewable energy sources, especially wind energy. The PTC has a built-in sunset clause, which means it must be renewed by congress every few years.

Key Industry Conferences and Events

One of the best ways for new employees in the energy industry to gain knowledge of the industry and learn about new technologies and developments is to attend industry conferences and events. In addition to gaining this valuable information, you will meet other employees and network with leaders in the industry, which can prove helpful as you develop your career path. Here are just a few of the key conferences and events in the energy industry today.

Coal-Gen is the largest event that covers the latest topics affecting the design, development, upgrading, operation, and maintenance of coal-fueled power plants. Occurring in August, the conference draws more than 4,500 industry professionals and 350 exhibitors. (http://www.coal-gen.com/index.html)

Distributech Conference and Exhibition takes place at the end of January or early February of each year. This conference focuses on Smart Grid technology: it covers automation and control systems, energy efficiency, demand response, renewable energy integration, advanced metering, transmission and distribution system operation and reliability, power delivery equipment, and water utility technology. (http://www.distributech.com/index.html)

Electric Light and Power Executive Conference invites industry executives from across the country to openly discuss the challenges and opportunities their companies are dealing with. Topics discussed include financing, policy, and integration of non-traditional fuel and energy sources. (http://www.elpconference.com/index.html)

Energypath is a weeklong event presented by the Sustainable Energy Fund. It is a fast-growing conference working to create a passion and understanding for sustainable energy in the leaders of today and tomorrow. Attendees learn from energy industry experts, policy makers, regulators and leading businesses. This event takes place in June. (http://energypath.org/energypath2011/Home.aspx)

Hydrovision International is a key industry event for the hydropower industry. It typically takes place in July and explores the issues affecting hydro resources. Another goal of this conference is to help participants develop a vision to meet challenges and ensure the future sustainability of hydropower. (http://www.hydroevent.com/index.html)

Municipal Solid Waste to Biofuels Summit is the first event to focus on building partnerships and securing funding to deliver full scale commercialization in the municipal waste to biofuels industry. (http://www.eyeforenergy.com/biofuels)

Nuclear Power International Conference usually occurs in December of each year and provides the nuclear power industry with a venue to gather and exchange information about nuclear power's rapidly changing role worldwide. (http://www.nuclear-powerinternational.com/index.html)

Power-Gen International is an annual conference that covers trends, technologies, and issues facing the generation sector, especially the need to operate more efficiently and cost-effectively. This conference typically takes place in December. (http://www.power-gen.com/index.html)

Solar Power International is an annual conference sponsored by the Solar Electric Power Association (SEPA) and the Solar Energy Industries Association. It provides a venue where the industry can come together with potential customers, policymakers, investors, and other parties necessary for continued rapid growth. The event, which occurs in October, draws more than 24,000 attendees. (http://www.solarpowerinternational.com)

Utility Products Conference takes place each February, bringing together the buyers and sellers of power, telecom, CATV, and water equipment to get the latest information and technology developments, as well as an opportunity to network. (http://www.utilityproductsexpo.com/index.html)

Windpower is produced by the American Wind Energy Association (AWEA). This conference, which takes place in May, provides a venue for the wind industry to network, do business, and solve problems. Nearly 1,400 exhibiting companies and thousands of wind energy professionals attend the event to take part in its educational information offerings and networking opportunities. (http://www.windpowerexpo.com)

World Hydrogen Technologies Convention meets each September. The International Association of Hydrogen Energy helps produce this event that focuses on exploring opportunities to create a clean, sustainable hydrogen economy from the many forms of available renewable energy. (http://www.whtc2011.org.uk)

Chapter 3

On the Job

There is a place for everyone in the energy industry. Although many jobs are highly technical or specialized, there are administrative positions, jobs for creative and innovative people, and jobs for people who are analytical and enjoy working with numbers.

Below you will find an A through Z listing of the jobs available in the energy industry. Each listing will describe the job, the education needed, if there are any direct reports associated with the job, the career path associated with it, as well as the salary range and whether there is certification or licensure required. With this information you can easily chart your path to your desired career result. For tips on how to best execute that plan, see Chapter 4, "Tips for Success".

Technical Positions

These are the essential positions of the industry, dealing with the extraction, transformation, and transportation of resources and energy.

Analytical Chemist

In the coal industry, the analytical chemist analyzes samples of an area's air, soil, and water to know their chemical composition. This allows the chemist to then determine whether a coal mine's operations have polluted the surrounding area. This position can also be called a research chemist. While some employers will hire a person with a bachelor's degree in science for an entry level position, most employers prefer chemists with a master's or doctoral degree as well as some experience in the industry, such as a number of years spent in both the lab and the field. In addition to an extensive knowledge of chemistry, analytical chemists should have good communication and organizational skills.

The analytical chemist typically does not have direct reports unless he or she is self-employed and has his or her own consulting firm. The average annual salary for analytical chemists is between $50,000 and $75,000, and could be higher or lower, depending on the position and location. In recent years the demand for analytical chemists has decreased due to an increase in automated sample testing and analysis systems. Now these chemists may find there is more opportunity in the field of quality assurance, or by starting their own consulting firms. While certification or licensure is not required to get a job as an analytical chemist, certification is offered through the National Registry of Certified Chemists and may give an employee a competitive edge. It may also be important for chemists who want to be self-employed consultants.

Chemist

Chemists often find positions in the nuclear energy industry. These chemists are needed to continually monitor the exterior and interior environments for radiation exposure. Outside, chemists test air, soil, and water samples for radiation; inside the power plant they test other materials. If unacceptable levels of radiation are discovered, the chemist coordinates the decontamination efforts.

Like the analytical chemist, a person with a bachelor's degree can get an entry-level chemist position, but most employers prefer chemists with a master's or doctoral degree and two to five years of experience in a nuclear power plant. In addition to having excellent problem solving and critical thinking skills, chemists should have an eye for detail and excellent computer skills. They must also be able to create succinct and accurate reports. Chemists usually do not have direct reports unless working for a multi-unit operation. In that situation, a chemist could supervise other chemists and lab personnel.

The average annual salary for chemists is between $50,000 and $75,000, and could be higher or lower, depending on the position and location. There are a few paths open to chemists. If the chemist wants to continue work in a nuclear power plant, he or she will need to be promoted into a management position. Another option is for the chemist to become an independent consultant to other plants. The third option is to work in research and development. Nuclear power companies usually look for chemists who have earned their certification through the National Registry of Certified Chemists.

Civil Engineer

Before engineering became highly specialized there were two kinds of engineers, those who worked for the military and those who worked for the public, or civil engineers. Civil engineers planned, designed, and helped construct public buildings, roads, bridges, and other structures and infrastructure used by a city or town. Today, the civil engineer in the energy industry focuses on structures used by energy producers, distributers, and retailers.

Most employers look for civil engineers who have at least a bachelor's degree in civil engineering, although many now prefer engineers that possess a master's degree. Civil engineers should also be both creative and analytical. They should possess good communication skills and be detail oriented. In some large companies, the civil engineer may have design assistants, interns, or administrative employees that report to him or her. In many instances, the engineer will not have direct reports.

The average annual salary for civil engineers is between $40,000 and $90,000, and could be higher or lower, depending on the position and location. In larger organizations, civil engineers can advance to senior engineers, supervisors, or managers. In smaller organizations they may become senior engineers or be responsible for more complex projects. In the United States, civil engineers must be licensed professional engineers. To become licensed, engineers must pass two types of exams, and in some states they must also work a number of years under the supervision of a licensed engineer. Requirements can vary from state to state. See Chapter 6 for resources that provide more information about licensing requirements.

Coal Gasification Engineer

A relatively new process, coal gasification is a way to mine underground veins of coal and convert it to a gas that can be used to produce heat or power. The gasification engineer plans, designs, constructs, and maintains the gasification equipment at a coal gasification plant. At a minimum, a bachelor's degree in mechanical engineering is required. Some employers prefer engineers with a master's or doctoral degree as well as several years of experience at a coal gasification plant and/or environmental engineering.

Coal gasification engineers should have very good communication skills, as well as the ability to work as part of a team. The engineer may have to give frequent presentations, so good presentation skills are also important. Coal gasification engineers usually do not have direct reports unless they are independent consultants. The average annual salary for coal gasification engineers is approximately $60,000. Some of these engineers earn as much as $100,000. There are two primary career paths open to coal gasification engineers: they can either become managers at the coal gasification plant, or they can be independent engineering consultants.

In the United States, all engineers must be licensed professional engineers. To become licensed, engineers must pass two types of exams, and in some states they must also work a number of years under the supervision of a licensed engineer. Requirements can vary from state to state. Web sites that offer more information about engineering licensing requirements can be found in Chapter 6.

Design Engineer (Renewable Energy)

In the renewable energy industry, design engineers design and develop new facilities for the production of renewable energy, or products and equipment necessary for that production. Design engineers do more than just design systems; they usually lead or coordinate entire projects. Most employers look for design engineers who have at least a bachelor's degree, although some prefer engineers that possess a master's degree.

The primary skill a design engineer should possess is excellent problem solving skills so that he or she can identify existing problems of current energy systems and improve upon the designs to correct them. Additionally, the design engineer should have good analytical skills to be able to identify issues and problems and an extensive knowledge of the renewable energy product business. Since the design engineer may lead a team of designers or other employees, he or she may have direct reports. The average annual salary for design engineers is between $50,000 and $100,000, and could be higher or lower, depending on the position and location.

If the design engineer works for an engineering firm, he or she could get promoted to project manager. Another career path for the

Fast Facts

Renewable Energy Alternatives

- There are now 60 geothermal power plants in five western United States: California, Nevada, Hawaii, Alaska, and Utah, with more under development.
- Wind energy can be used in nearly 50 percent of the country, but it is more widely used in Europe than it is here.
- Solar energy could generate 2.5 percent of the world's electricity by 2025.

design engineer is to work as an independent consultant, or he or she could be hired by a renewable energy production facility. In the United States, engineers must be licensed professional engineers. To become licensed, engineers must pass two exams, and in some states they must also work a number of years under the supervision of a licensed engineer. Requirements can vary from state to state. Web sites that offer more information about engineering licensing requirements can be found in Chapter 6.

Electrical Engineer

Electrical engineers can work in a variety of industries, and usually their task is to test, improve, or design electrical products or equipment. In the electric power industry, the electrical engineer helps to design electrical delivery systems, whether at the generating side or the transmission side. The electrical engineer may need to design service to a new housing development, large commercial structure, or a new generating plant.

Most employers look for electrical engineers who have at least a bachelor's degree in electrical engineering, although a master's degree may be preferred in certain situations or jobs. Electrical engineers should have excellent technical skills, as well as excellent communication skills. They should also have good computer skills and be able to work as part of a team. These skills are required because these engineers will use computer design programs in their daily work, and will also need to effectively communicate their design instructions to construction workers. In most cases the electrical engineer will not have direct reports. The average annual salary for electrical engineers is between $45,000 and $95,000. In larger organizations, electrical engineers can advance to senior engineers, supervisors, or project managers. In smaller organizations they may become senior engineers or be responsible for more complex projects. Electrical engineers must be licensed professional engineers. To become licensed, engineers must pass two exams, and in some states they must also work a number of years under the supervision of a licensed engineer. Requirements can vary from state to state. More information about engineering licensure can be found in Chapter 6.

Electric Construction Worker

In some large electric utility companies in which there is a lot of ongoing construction taking place, electric line workers work full time on construction products. These construction projects can range from installing electric lines to new housing developments to three-phase electrical transmission service to a large factory. (Three-phase service is most often utilized by large consumers of electricity or those that require a higher voltage than residential consumers; the service is provided in three different levels of voltages, so that the customer can utilize higher or lower voltages as needed.) These construction workers specialize in constructing new service rather than repairing existing service.

In most electric power companies electric construction workers need to have a high school diploma and several years of experience working as a line worker at a utility company. Due to the advent of the Smart Grid and other high technology plans for the electric utility system, more employers are looking for line workers that have more technical skills and experience. Many technical schools and community colleges are offering associate degree programs or certification programs for electric line technicians.

This can be a physically demanding job, so the construction worker should be able to lift heavy objects as well as climb poles and run specialized construction equipment. The construction worker must be able to work as part of a team and have good communication skills.

The average annual salary for line construction workers is between $44,000 and $60,000. Construction workers just starting out can earn as low as $27,000 per year. Construction workers can become crew supervisor, and eventually a manager. The worker will need to earn a college degree in order to advance past this position. There are no certifications or licenses required for this position. In most utility companies, non-management workers are expected to join the labor union, which advocates for them in terms of pay, time off, and benefits.

Electric Line Personnel (Installation and Repair)

If the electric line worker is not on a permanent construction crew, he or she handles small installation projects and repairs to the distribution lines. For example, electric line crews replace poles that are aging, replace lines that need to be upgraded, or repair lines that have been damaged due to vehicle accidents or storms.

In most electric power companies electric line workers need to have a high school diploma and some experience working as a line worker at a utility company. Due to the advent of the Smart Grid and other high technology plans for the electric utility system, more employers are looking for line workers that have more technical skills and experience. Many technical schools and community colleges are offering associate degree programs or certification programs for electric line technicians.

Like the electric construction worker position, this can be a physically demanding job, so the electric line worker should be able to lift heavy objects as well as climb poles and run specialized construction equipment. The line worker may have more contact with customers so should have good communication and customer service skills.

The average annual salary for line workers is between $44,000 and $60,000. Line workers just starting out can earn as low as $27,000 per year. The line worker can be promoted to supervisor, but will need to earn a four-year degree to become a manager or other administrative position. There are no certifications or licenses required for the electric line worker. In most utility companies, non-management workers are expected to join the labor union, which advocates for them in terms of pay, time off, and benefits.

Electric Service/Line Supervisor

The electric line or service supervisor supervises the line crew and/ or electric service crew for a particular location of the utility company. This person assigns the work for each day and ensures that all projects and work are getting completed on time and within budget. The supervisor is also expected to supervise crews when there are outages.

In some companies the supervisor will need to have a bachelor's degree in electrical engineering or business, while other companies promote exceptional line crew workers into this position. However, once promoted, the supervisor may be expected to get a degree. Excellent leadership skills are required. The supervisor must also have a great deal of knowledge of the electric utility system and how it functions, excellent communication skills and good problem solving skills.

As a supervisor, this person will have a number of direct reports, depending on the size of the department and its location. Some supervisors have eight to 10 workers he or she will supervise, while others may have 40 or 50 workers. The average annual salary for line supervisors is between $40,000 and $90,000, depending on the number of workers he or she will supervise and the size of the service area. As long as the supervisor has his or her bachelor's degree, the supervisor could be promoted to service center manager, project manager, or other management position. There is no certification or license required for this position.

Electric Service Technician

The electric service technician is similar to a line worker, except that the service technician is responsible for repairing and investigating the customer's electric problems. The service tech may be called to investigate why a customer's electric bill is unusually high, or why the customer is experiencing a lack of power in part of his or her home. Rather than working strictly on the distribution lines and installation projects, this is a hands-on customer service position.

In most electric power companies, electric service techs need to have a high school diploma and some experience working with electric systems. The increasing complexity of electrical system technology is creating an increased demand for service workers with more technical skills and experience. Many technical schools and community colleges are offering associate degree programs or certification programs for electric line technicians and workers. Service techs should have excellent problem solving skills as well as very good knowledge of electrical systems within a customer's home or business. They should also have good communication and customer service skills. The service technician does not have direct reports.

The average annual salary for service technicians is between $34,000 and $60,000. Some companies will promote excellent service techs into supervisory positions. However, once in that role he or she may be required to get his or her degree. A degree will be required for any other management, engineering, or administrative position. There are no certifications or licenses required for the electric line worker. In most utility companies, non-management workers are expected to join the labor union. These unions negotiate with company management employees to determine the union workers' pay, time off, and benefits.

Engineering Technicians

Engineering technicians are employed in many segments of the energy industry, but they are very common in electric power utility companies. Engineering technicians assist the electrical engineer. While the engineer is responsible for the overall project—from initial design to final construction—the engineer does a lot of the hands-on research and data gathering needed to create the design of the project. The engineering tech also drafts the plans using computer-aided design, and may inspect and test equipment during the project.

Engineering technicians can find employment with an associate's degree in engineering technology from an accredited technical school or college. Techs can earn a bachelor's degree in engineering if he or she plans to advance to engineer. Engineering technicians should have excellent problem solving skills, an eye for detail, and good communication skills. In some positions, creativity may also be required. The engineering technician does not have direct reports.

The average annual salary for engineering technicians is between $40,000 and $60,000. The natural career path for engineering techs is to become an engineer. If he or she does not have a degree, this can take up to 10 years of work and experience to prove he or she has the knowledge required to be an engineer. Certification is not required to get a job, but there is certification available for tech engineers that can give them a competitive edge over other candidates competing for the same job. Certification can be obtained through the National Institute for Certification in Engineering Technologies (http://www.nicet.org).

Environmental Engineer

The environmental engineer's primary concern is the effect of energy projects on the environment. The engineer looks at the location for the project, and assesses the impacts the operations of the facility will have on the surrounding area. If needed, the engineer proposes steps to be taken to safeguard the environment or remediate if an impact has occurred.

Most employers look for environmental engineers who have at least a bachelor's degree in mechanical, civil, environmental, or chemical engineering, although many now prefer engineers that possess a master's degree. Environmental engineers should have excellent problem solving skills, decision making, and critical thinking skills. They should also have very good communication and interpersonal skills. The environmental engineer may have a technician that reports to him or her, but most likely there will be no direct reports. The salary range for environmental engineers is between $50,000 and $115,000, although the average salary is around $77,000 per year. Environmental engineers can work for government agencies or for engineering firms. In the firm, the engineer can become a senior engineer. At government agencies there are usually predetermined career paths for engineers, depending on the agency. They could become managers or other administrators.

Environmental engineers are not required to be licensed professional engineers like other engineers, but it can give an environmental engineer a competitive edge if he or she does become licensed. To become licensed, engineers must pass two types of exams, and in some states they must also work a number of years under the supervision of a licensed engineer. Requirements can vary from state to state. More information about engineering licensure can be found in Chapter 6.

Geologist

Geologists work in two segments of the energy industry: coal production, and petroleum exploration. In both cases, the geologist uses his or her scientific knowledge of the Earth as well as sophisticated equipment and samples to determine a location of either veins of coal or oil so that a company can extract it.

While some entry-level jobs may accept applicants with a bachelor's degree in geology, geotechnical engineering, or mining engineering, the majority of jobs require a master's degree in geology or earth science. High-level positions will require a doctoral degree. In addition to their scientific expertise, geologists should have excellent time management skills, strong analytical thinking skills, and excellent communication skills.

The average annual salary for geologists in the oil and coal industry is between $75,000 and $100,000. Geologists working for the government earn an average annual salary of $90,000 per year. There are three main career paths for geologists. They could be promoted to manager of mines or oil refineries. In a government position there will be structured advancement in pay and responsibilities. To earn more money and have more responsibilities the geologist could become an independent consultant. Most states require that geologists receive a license from a state licensing board, although not every state does.

Geophysicist

Like geologists, geophysicists also use their scientific knowledge and available technology to determine where oil is likely to be located in the Earth. The primary difference between geophysicists and geologists is that the geophysicist studies the interior of the Earth, while geologists study soils, rocks, and other surface materials.

Like the geologist, geophysicists may be able to get entry-level jobs with a bachelor's degree in geology or geotechnical engineering, but most jobs will require a master's degree in geology or earth science. In order to perform research, geophysicists will need to earn a doctoral degree. Geophysicists must have excellent analytical thinking skills, excellent written and oral communication skills, and a strong science background and computer skills. Most geophysicists will not have direct reports.

The average annual salary for geophysicists in the oil industry is between $75,000 and $100,000. Geophysicists working for the government earn an average annual salary of $90,000 per year. If the geophysicist works for a for-profit company, he or she may not be able to advance beyond working on projects with more responsibility. Most geophysicists choose to work for the government or academic institutions, while others start their own consulting firms. Some states require that geophysicists become licensed through the state licensing board. To become licensed the geophysicist may have to take an exam and/or work a certain number of years in the field.

Geoscience Technician

The geoscience technician works with the geologist or engineer to gather data, create maps, and help make recommendations about where veins of coal or petroleum are located. A lot of his or her time will be spent gathering and analyzing data and putting it together to create reports and recommendations. An associate's degree in computer science, earth science, or geology may be sufficient for a person to get a position as a geosciences technician. Most employers, though, prefer technicians that have a bachelor degree in one of these areas of study. Geoscience technicians must have very strong computer skills, data analysis skills, and decision-making skills. He or she should also have very good written and interpersonal communication skills so he or she will be making presentations and writing reports.

The average annual salary range for geoscience technicians is between $25,000 and $60,000, depending on the position and how much experience he or she has in the industry. If a geoscience technician wants to advance in this line of work, he or she will need to gain more education. If he or she does not already have a bachelor degree he or she will need to obtain one, as well as a master's degree. There are no licenses or certifications required for geoscience technicians.

Health Physicist

Health physicists can work for the government and other organizations to help protect an environment from radiation exposure. In the energy industry, the health physicist works at a nuclear power plant to protect employees from getting too much radiation exposure. That means he or she chooses the proper equipment and devices for radiation prevention. They also must know all federal and state safety and environmental regulations for radiation and ensure that the nuclear plant is always in compliance.

The health physicist can get a job at a nuclear power plant with a bachelor's degree in physics, chemistry, engineering, or radiation biology, or occupational health. However, more employers are looking to fill these positions with people who have master's or doctoral degrees. Health physicists must be highly technical, able to analyze data, be detail oriented, and have very good interpersonal and written communication skills. In most positions, the health physicist will not have other employees reporting to him or her.

The average annual salary range for health physicists is between $55,000 and $95,000 or more. This is quite a wide range. Health physicists with more education and experience will earn the higher salaries. Career options for health physicists include becoming researchers or academic instructors (for health physicists with advanced degrees) or independent consultants. Health physicists must become certified. Certification may be obtained through the American Board of Health Physics (http://www.hps1.org/aahp/boardweb/abhphome.html).

Instrument Technician

There are a few segments of the energy industry that hire instrument technicians. Instrument technicians work on oil rigs, in power plants, and in nuclear power plants. Although the equipment they work on will vary in each of these employment locations, the basic job remains the same. Their main responsibility is to inspect, test, adjust, and repair all control systems and equipment. It is vital to the operation that these systems are functioning properly.

In some positions, the instrument technician can be hired with a high school diploma, but most employers seek people with an associate's degree in applied science, electrical engineering technology or electronics. A bachelor's degree is usually not necessary. Strong mechanical skills are required. These technicians should also have good communication skills as well as computer skills. The instrument technician will not have direct reports.

The average annual salary range for instrument technicians is between $45,000 and $65,000, depending on which segment of the energy industry he or she works in and how many years of experience he or she has. If the technician earns his or her bachelor's degree in engineering or even a master's degree, he or she can become an electrical or mechanical engineer. To work in an electric or nuclear power plant, the instrument technician will need to be certified as a mechanical or electrical technician.

Machine Operators

Machine operators are mostly hired in the coal mining industry. Whether the employer is surface mining or mining underground, there are many machines that require operators. The various machines convey the coal, cut the coal, load coal onto other machines, distribute rock dust, drill blastholes, and scoop away the earth.

To become machine operators in coal mines, workers are required to have a high school diploma. Most operators start out as apprentice operators, working under more experienced operators for a year or two before working on their own. Machine operators must be physically fit, have good manual dexterity, some machine and technical skills, and good communication skills. Machine operators will not have direct reports. More experienced operators may be in charge of training the apprentices.

The average annual salary range for machine operators is between $30,000 and $65,000. More experienced operators with seniority typically earn the higher salaries. Operators with a broader range of experience in the mine can become health and safety inspectors. They can also be promoted to supervisor positions, although they will need to work several years before this may happen. For positions such as an administrative or management position, the operator will need to earn a bachelor's degree. Most of the states in the country require mining employees to earn certification through the Miners' Examining Board. Requirements for certification vary from state to state, but most include a course in mining safety and rescue.

Materials Engineer

Materials engineers can work in many industries. In the energy industry they are often hired by nuclear energy production facilities to analyze the materials that are required to build a plant. The materials engineer's goal is to ensure that the building materials used will be adequate for the conditions needed to create nuclear energy.

Most employers look for materials engineers who have at least a bachelor's degree in materials science, metallurgy, or chemistry, although many now prefer engineers that possess a master's degree. Materials engineers should have excellent problem solving skills, decision making, and critical thinking skills. They should also have excellent computer skills and oral and written communication skills. Materials engineers usually do not have direct reports.

The average annual salary for materials engineers is approximately $80,000. To advance their careers, materials engineers could join private research firms, become independent consultants, or work for the government. If they continue to work for the nuclear energy industry they could become senior technical managers. In the United States, materials engineers must be licensed professional engineers. To become licensed, engineers must pass two types of exams, and in some states they must also work a number of years under the supervision of a licensed engineer. Requirements can vary from state to state. More information about engineering licensure can be found in Chapter 6.

Mechanical Engineer

The mechanical engineer is an important person to many companies and various industries. The mechanical engineer is especially important to the energy industry, where he or she helps to design and plan engines and power-producing machines and equipment in the power plant. They also perform analyses on existing machines and make recommendations for improvements or corrections.

Most employers look for mechanical engineers who have at least a bachelor's degree in mechanical engineering, although many now prefer engineers that possess a master's degree. Mechanical engineers must have extensive knowledge of federal, state, and local safety codes. They also should have excellent problem solving skills, decision making, and critical thinking skills. Mechanical engineers should also have strong computer skills as well as good communication skills and the ability to work well as part of a team. In some large companies, the mechanical engineer may have design assistants, interns, or administrative employees that report to him or her. In many instances, the engineer will not have direct reports.

The average annual salary for mechanical engineers is between $77,000 and $85,000, and could be higher or lower, depending on the position and location. In larger organizations, mechanical engineers can advance to senior engineers, supervisors, or managers. In smaller organizations they may become senior engineers or be responsible for more complex projects. In the United States, mechanical engineers must be licensed professional engineers. To become licensed, engineers must pass two exams, and in some states they must also work a number of years under the supervision of a licensed engineer. See Chapter 6 for more information about engineering licensure.

Mine Inspectors

The mine inspector position is considered a low level supervisory or management job. The inspector is in charge of ensuring that the mine is meeting all of its contractual agreements, as well as all federal, state, and local safety requirements. To do this, the inspector thoroughly examines all aspects of the mine's operations, looking for areas that may become dangerous to employees. For example, the inspector might find rotten support structures or poor air quality.

Most employers hire mine inspectors who have at least a bachelor's degree in engineering, although many now prefer employees that possess a master's degree. Mine inspectors should have extensive knowledge of all federal, state, and local safety regulations. He or she should also have excellent problem solving, decision making, and critical thinking skills, as well as good leadership and supervisory skills. While the mine inspector may not have direct reports, he or she does have the authority to discipline or instruct employees who are not following safety procedures.

The average annual salary for mine inspectors is approximately $56,000. Inspectors with several years of experience could earn higher salaries. As long as the mine inspector holds a bachelor's degree, the usual career path is to become a mine safety engineer (see below). Most of the states in the country require mining employees to earn certification through the Miners' Examining Board. Requirements for certification vary from state to state, but most include a course in mining safety and rescue. Professional engineer certification is necessary for higher-level supervisory positions.

Mine Safety Engineer

Similar to the mine inspector, the primary goal of the mine safety engineer is to ensure that a mine is meeting all federal, state, and local safety laws, regulations, and requirements. The mine safety engineer will test air samples, equipment, and perform other tests necessary to ensure compliance and safety. The mine safety engineer will also train other mine employees in all aspects of safety.

Most employers look for mine safety engineers who have at least a bachelor's degree in mining engineering, although many now prefer engineers that possess a master's degree in a specialized engineering field. Mine safety engineers should have an aptitude for math and science, excellent communication skills, both in conversation and writing, good investigative and leadership skills, and excellent computer skills. In some large companies, the mine safety engineer may have mine inspectors or other supervisors who report to him or her.

The average annual salary for mine safety engineers is approximately $76,000, and could be higher or lower depending on experience. There are scant ways for a mine safety engineer to advance if he or she is working in a coal mine, since there are no senior positions in this field. In order to earn more money and gain more knowledge and responsibility, the mine safety engineer will need to become an independent consultant or form an engineering firm with other kinds of engineers.

In the United States, engineers must be licensed professional engineers. To become licensed, engineers must pass two types of exams, and in some states they must also work a number of years under the supervision of a licensed engineer. Requirements can vary from state to state. More information about engineering and mining licensure can be found in Chapter 6. Most of the states in the country also require mining employees to earn certification through the Miners' Examining Board. Requirements for certification vary from state to state, but most include a course in mining safety and rescue. Professional engineer certification is also necessary for mine safety engineers.

Best Practice

Choosing the Right Job in the Energy Industry

There are many factors that play into the decision of what career to embark on. The first thing anyone should do when trying to choose a career is to do some research: find out what the salary range is, what education and training are required, who the top employers are, and what the job responsibilities are. The best way to determine if a job will work is to talk to others that are doing the job now, and actually try the job out by shadowing them. There are also several books and Web sites that offer quizzes and evaluate skills and interests of a person in order to determine a career choice best suited for that person. Take a look at *Career Tests: 25 Revealing Self-Tests to Help You Find and Succeed at the Perfect Career* by Louis H. Janda, or the popular Web sites Free-Career-Tes.com and LiveCareer.com.

Mining Engineer

Mining engineers are essential employees to a coal mine's operations. They are responsible for finding, extracting, and preparing the
coal for use by power companies. The engineers fulfill this responsibility by conducting surveys of the various coal deposits found
in a mine and testing them as well as their locations to determine
whether they are worth the time, expense, and effort of mining.
They also supervise the construction of mine shafts.

Mining engineers must have at least a bachelor's degree in mining engineering, although many employers now prefer engineers
that possess a master's degree. Mining engineers should have excellent problem solving skills, decision making, analytical, and critical thinking skills. They should also have strong interpersonal and
communication skills, as well as familiarity with computer design
software and tools. In some mines, the mining engineer will have
direct reports that include the mine safety inspector and engineer or
other mining employees.

The average annual salary for mining engineers is approximately
$76,000, and could be higher or lower, depending on the position
and location. In larger organizations, entry-level mining engineers
work to become more senior engineers, which allows them to work
on more complex projects. They also may supervise a staff of engineers or technical workers. In the United States, engineers must be
licensed professional engineers. To become licensed, engineers must
pass two types of exams, and in some states they must also work
a number of years under the supervision of a licensed engineer.
Requirements can vary from state to state. More information about
engineering and mining licensure can be found in Chapter 6.

Nuclear Engineer

The nuclear engineer works for nuclear power plants or companies
that produce nuclear power. The engineer's main task is to design,
develop, and monitor nuclear power plants. They oversee the construction of new facilities and conduct tests to assess the plant's
capabilities. Most employers look for nuclear engineers who hold
both a bachelor's degree in nuclear engineering as well as a master's
degree in mathematics, physics, or a related field.

Nuclear engineers should have a high degree of creativity and
ingenuity. They should also be detail oriented, be able to work as
part of a team, have good time management and organizational

skills, and also effective oral and written communication skills. In some companies, the nuclear engineer will have one or more nuclear technicians working under him or her. These technicians are recent college graduates looking for experience under the supervision of the more experienced nuclear engineer.

The average annual salary for nuclear engineers is approximately $100,000. If the nuclear engineer continues to work for the nuclear power company, his or her next position would be nuclear plant supervisor. Otherwise, to advance his or her career the nuclear engineer will need to take a research position with a private company, academic institution or a position within the government. In the United States, nuclear engineers must be licensed professional engineers. To become licensed, engineers must pass two types of exams, and in some states they must also work a number of years under the supervision of a licensed engineer. For more information about engineering licensure, see Chapter 6.

Nuclear Monitoring Technician

One of the primary focuses of the nuclear monitoring technician is the amount of radiation employees are being exposed to through working at the nuclear power plant. The nuclear monitoring technician monitors the amount of radiation present. He or she may also assist the nuclear engineer or nuclear physicist in their work.

A high school diploma or associate's degree in science is usually the level of education required for this position, although some employers may prefer to hire a person with a bachelor's degree in science. Technicians will also work three to five years under a more experienced technician before working on his or her own. Nuclear monitoring technicians must have long attention spans, be very detail oriented, and have the capacity to follow detailed instructions. They also need excellent communication and organizational skills. Nuclear monitoring technicians usually do not have direct reports. More senior technicians may train new technicians.

The average annual salary range for nuclear engineering technicians is between $35,000 and $70,000. New technicians earn the smallest salaries. The typical career path leads technicians to the health physicist, nuclear engineer, or nuclear plant supervisor position after many years of experience and additional education. Most nuclear technicians need to be certified. Certification can be obtained through the Nuclear Medicine Technology Certification

Board (http://www.nmtcb.org), and the American Registry of Radiologic Technologists (http://www.arrt.org). This usually entails taking classes and passing an exam.

Nuclear Physicist

The nuclear physicist is concerned less with the actual operation of a nuclear power plant and more with how to construct one that operates more efficiently or improving the efficiency of an existing plant. While nuclear engineers design and construct the plant, the nuclear physicist is continually conducting research and tests to create new and improved methods for creating nuclear energy.

While some physicists may be able to obtain a position with a bachelor's degree, most employers seek nuclear physicists with a master's or doctorate degree. Since most physicists work in an academic setting, a doctorate degree is recommended. Nuclear physicists should have excellent analytical skills, problem solving skills, decision making, and critical thinking skills. They should also have very solid computer skills as well as imagination, initiative, and creativity. In some academic and research positions, the nuclear physicist could have research assistants or administrative personnel reporting to him or her.

The average annual salary for nuclear physicists is between $50,000 and $110,000. This salary can be higher for physicists working for the government or in military positions. In nuclear power plants, the natural progression for the nuclear physicist is to become a nuclear engineer. However, many physicists choose to work in an academic setting or for the government, where they can conduct research, have greater responsibilities, and earn higher salaries. If the physicist decides to work in an academic setting, he or she will need to become certified to teach in the state where he or she works. Each state has different requirements for certification for teachers.

Nuclear Reactor Operators

A nuclear power plant must be staffed and run 24 hours a day. The nuclear reactor is the main device for creating the energy that will be used by the customer. It is also very important for the reactor to be working within safe parameters. The nuclear reactor operators are the workers who staff the control room and equipment outside the control room to keep the plant running smoothly. Operators that work outside of the control room are called auxiliary reactor operators, while operators who supervise other operators are senior reactor operators.

To become a nuclear reactor operator, it is necessary to have a high school diploma, after having taken advanced math and science courses, as well as several years of experience in the nuclear energy or related industry. A person can also become an operator with a two-year or four year college degree in a related field. Operators need to be able to read technical diagrams and reports. They should also have manual dexterity, mechanical abilities, and good technical and computer skills. The senior nuclear reactor operator will supervise the other operators on his or her shift, including trainees. The other operators will not have direct reports.

The average annual salary for nuclear reactor operators varies widely, depending on whether the person is a trainee, an operator, or a senior operator. New operators and trainees can start out with a salary of around $25,000 per year, while senior operators can earn up to $150,000 per year. Operators that want to remain in that area of the industry can start out as trainees and work their way up to senior nuclear reactor operator. The senior operator can become promoted to senior supervisor of plant operations. The U.S. Nuclear Regulatory Commission (NRC) requires that all operators become licensed. To get a license, the operator must pass a physical exam and take and pass a written exam given by the NRC. The operator will need to have received his or her education and training prior to taking the exam.

Performance Engineer

The performance engineer works primarily for the electric utility company. His or her primary function is to test the performance of the generation, transmission, and distribution of the electricity the company produces. He or she conducts tests at the power plant, substations, and on distribution lines, and recommends actions to improve the performance of the transmission and delivery of electric service to the customers.

Some performance engineers with a bachelor's degree in electrical or mechanical engineering and several years of experience can get jobs in the electric utility industry, although many employers now prefer engineers that possess a master's degree. Performance engineers should have excellent communication skills, be knowl-edgeable of measurement and benchmarking methods, and have excellent problem solving skills and project management skills. In some large companies, performance engineers may have electrical engineers or engineering technicians that report to him or her. How-ever, often the performance engineer will not have direct reports.

The average annual salary range for performance engineers is between $50,000 and $95,000. In the electric utility industry, per-formance engineers have the ability to be promoted to power plant management positions or power plant system operators. In the United States, performance engineers must be licensed professional engineers. Engineers must pass two types of exams and in some states they must also work a number of years under the supervision of a licensed engi-neer. Requirements for licensure can vary from state to state. More information about engineering licensure can be found in Chapter 6.

Petroleum Engineer

There are three primary petroleum engineering jobs. Drilling engi-neers work as part of a team of geologists and construction per-sonnel and contractors to design, plan, and construct new drilling operations. The goal of production engineers is to improve or correct

Professional
Ethics

How to Resign from a New Job

It does not happen often—but it does happen. You accept a job thinking it is your ideal position, only to find out after a week or two that it is nothing like you thought it would be. How can you tactfully resign without damaging your reputation? Human resource experts agree that in every situa-tion honesty is the best policy. Let the boss know as soon as possible that the job is not what you had expected. Do not lay blame on the company because you do not want to burn any bridges. The sooner you resign, the more likely the company can hire a replacement that was already interviewed, preventing them from having to start all over with the recruiting and hiring process.

existing equipment to maintain or enhance oil production. The reservoir engineer's focus is on improving performance of each drilling operation and predicting each drilling operation's output.

While some engineers with a bachelor's degree in petroleum engineering and several years of experience in the industry can get one of these jobs, most employers prefer to hire petroleum engineers who have a master's or doctorate degree. Petroleum engineers need to have excellent problem solving, decision making, and analytical/critical thinking skills. They need to be able to work as part of a team and have excellent communication skills. Most petroleum engineers will not have direct reports. However, if they are promoted to engineering team lead or another management position he or she will have direct reports.

The average annual salary for petroleum engineers is between $48,000 and $140,000. Assistant engineers and technicians make the lower salaries. Petroleum engineers may start out as engineering technicians or assistants. They can then be promoted to engineer, and to advance their careers further, they can become engineering team leader or another management position. They can also advance their careers by starting their own consulting business. Registration or licensing may be required, depending on the state in which the operation is located.

Pipe Fitter

The pipe fitter is a worker that specializes in the laying out, assembling, fabricating, and maintenance of the pipes used to convey steam in a nuclear power plant. Pipe fitters can also work in the natural gas industry and petroleum industry, working on the pipes that transport natural gas or oil. Pipe fitters will need to have a high school diploma or GED, and need to complete an apprenticeship, or a specific training period in which the pipe fitter works under the supervision of a more experienced employee. Candidates for the job must be physically strong, have manual dexterity, and have good communication skills. Pipe fitters should also have good math skills and time management and problem solving skills. The pipe fitter does not have direct reports, unless he or she is promoted to a supervisory position.

There is quite a large salary range for pipe fitters. Apprentice pipe fitters can start out earning as little as $19,000 per year and senior pipe fitters and supervisors earn as much as $70,000 or higher. Pipe fitters start out as apprentices, and then are able to work on their own. To advance their careers they can become supervisors or become self-employed or consultants. Some states in the United States require pipe fitters to become licensed or certified. Each state will have different requirements for licensing.

Power Distributor and Dispatcher

Power distributors and dispatchers are the workers endeavoring to ensure there is plenty of power available when customers' demand increases due to changes in the weather or other factors. These distributors monitor the power being generated at various plants and contact plant operators to shut down generators or bring them online as demand fluctuates. Although a high school graduate can become a power distributor or dispatcher, many plants are looking for employees with a bachelor degree in science. It is critical for power distributors to have excellent decision making skills and be highly responsible and responsive to the demands of the job. If the distributor does not respond appropriately it could result in a brown out or other consequences. They should also have excellent communication skills, be knowledgeable of the electric generation and distribution systems, and be detail oriented. Paying close attention to all the factors that affect demand and communicating them to the appropriate personnel will mean that power generation will meet demand. The power plant distributor or dispatcher does not have any direct reports unless he or she has been promoted to supervisor.

Beginning distributors, or apprentices, start out earning approximately $38,000 per year, while senior distributors or supervisors can make as much as $80,000. Employees start out as electric power systems apprentices or mechanical technicians. They are then promoted to the position of power distributor and dispatcher. To advance further, employees can be promoted to power plant supervisor or shift supervisor. Employees who want to work as power distributors or dispatchers must earn certification as either a fireman or engineer. Which certification the employee needs and how he or she will go about obtaining it will vary from state to state. The employee will need to check with his or her state's licensing agency.

Power Plant Operator

The power plant operator is in charge of operating the equipment at a power plant or generating plant, usually through a control board.

This equipment can include boilers, turbines, generators, and other pieces of equipment and machinery. Working with the distribution and dispatch workers, they start and stop turbines and generators according to the demand for electricity. A high school diploma is usually all that is required to become a power plant operator, although some employers have begun to look for employees with a bachelor's degree. The operator starts out as a technician and works for several years before becoming an operator.

A power plant operator must be able to prioritize and manage several projects. He or she should also have excellent communication skills, problem solving skills, good manual dexterity, and a degree of physical fitness. A power plant operator may be in charge of training or working with mechanical technicians; otherwise, he or she will not have any direct reports unless promoted to supervisor. Operators start out as mechanical technicians, earning about $30,000 per year. Senior power plant operators and supervisors can earn as much as $70,000 per year. After working as a power plant operator for a number of years, the employee can then be promoted to power plant supervisor or shift supervisor. Power plant operators will not usually need to be licensed or certified. However, it may be recommended for them to join a union, which advocates for them in terms of pay, time off, and benefits.

Solar Engineer

The solar engineer works with a team of other scientists and engineers to develop, design, and construct solar energy systems. Since current solar power systems are not as efficient as other forms of power production, solar engineers conduct experiments and research to find new methods and materials that will improve the efficiency of solar energy production. Most employers look for solar engineers who have at least a bachelor's degree in chemical, electrical, environmental, or mechanical engineering, although many now prefer engineers that possess a master's degree.

Solar engineers should have excellent analytical thinking skills, problem solving skills, the ability to make informed decisions, and be creative and innovative in order to identify areas for improvement on solar energy production designs. They should also have excellent communication and presentation skills as well as project and time management skills, since they must juggle multiple priorities and frequently make presentations. Solar engineers usually do not have direct reports.

The average annual salary range for solar engineers is between $30,000 and $105,000. Engineering technicians just starting out will earn the lower salaries, while senior engineers will earn the higher salaries. Solar engineers usually start out as engineering technicians right after graduating from college. After working as technicians for a period of time and gaining valuable knowledge and experience, they can become solar engineers. To advance their careers, they will need to become project managers or independent consultants. Engineers need to be licensed professional engineers. To become licensed, engineers must pass two exams, and in some states they must also work a number of years under the supervision of a licensed engineer. More information about engineering licensure can be found in Chapter 6.

Solar Power Installer

Solar polar installers do what the job title indicates: they install solar power panels and systems in homes, businesses, or for large commercial or industrial facilities. Solar power installers are becoming more and more in demand and it takes some education and training to become a certified installer. Most solar power installers must at least have a high school diploma or GED. However, technical schools and community colleges often have associate's degree programs or certification programs for energy industry jobs such as installer. Employers are more likely to hire a graduate of one of these programs than candidates who do not have any formal training. Solar power installers must be physically fit, have good manual dexterity, and not be afraid of heights. They should also have good decision-making skills, and be able to work with a team. Installers usually do not have direct reports unless they become supervisors.

The average annual salary range for solar power installers is between $41,000 and $60,000. Some new installers could earn less, while supervisors could earn higher salaries. Solar power installers can advance their careers by becoming crew supervisors. They can also become solar power sales technicians and earn more money and become eligible for other promotions. Solar power installers will want to become certified through the National Board of Certified Energy Practitioners (NABCEP). The NABCEP is the highest level of certification available in the United States for workers in this field. To get this certification installers need to have a combination of experience, training and or education, and take and pass an exam. More information can be found at Nabcep.org.

Welder

A welder is considered a skilled labor position in many different industries, including many segments of the energy industry. Welders are needed for the fabrication and repair of equipment, pipes, machines, and other materials. Welders use hand-welding and flame-cutting equipment to melt metals and join them together or to fill holes and seams. High school graduates can get jobs as welders in many industries. Most new welders, however, will need to get technical training or complete an apprenticeship before they are able to work independently. Welders need to have good eyesight, good eye-hand coordination, manual dexterity, and be in good shape physically. They should also be detail oriented. Welders do not have direct reports unless they have been promoted to supervisor.

The average annual salary range for welders is between $20,000 and $50,000. Apprentices earn the salaries on the low end of the range, while supervisors can earn the higher salaries. Welders start out as apprentices, and work under the supervision of senior welders. Once the apprenticeship is over, they work as welders independently. The next promotion a welder can earn is that of supervisor. Welders can also potentially earn more money as independent contractors. Welders are required to become certified through the American Welding Society. To learn more about the certification process, visit Aws.org.

Wind Turbine Technician

The wind turbine technician is responsible for maintaining and servicing commercial scale wind turbines used in energy production. The technicians typically work in teams of two to ensure each other's safety. This position combines knowledge of mechanics, hydraulics, meteorology, and computer skills with manual dexterity and physical strengths and abilities. Today most community colleges and technical schools offer training, associate's degree programs, or certification programs for wind energy technicians. These programs usually offer a combination of classroom experiences and hands-on laboratory work in which students actually service and maintain wind turbines.

Since wind turbines can be taller than 200 feet, it is essential for technicians to be comfortable with heights. Technicians will also need to have excellent problem solving and decision-making skills and extensive knowledge of wind turbine machinery and safety regulations and requirements. Wind turbine technicians will not have direct reports unless they have been promoted to a supervisory position.

The average hourly wage for wind turbine technicians is between $16 and $30, depending on where the job is located and how much experience the technician has. Jobs in more highly populated areas usually pay higher salaries. New wind turbine technicians may need to work as an apprentice or assistant for a minimal amount of time. Soon the technician will work with another technician to service the turbines. To advance his or her career he or she can become a team lead, supervisor, trainer, or work at an academic institution to provide education and training to students. Certification for wind turbine technicians is available, but not a requirement to obtain a job. For more information, see Nabcep.org.

Business or Administrative Positions

In addition to the industry-specific jobs listed earlier, there are many other professional, business, or administrative positions that are necessary in the energy industry and many of them are common to all businesses. Here are a few of them, along with their importance to the energy industry.

Accountant

Accounting is an important function for any operation, large or small. Often accounts tie in to inventory, human resource management, and other measurements of operational efficiency. Accountants look at all aspects of an operation in conjunction with their budget numbers—how much the department costs the business, as well as whether it brings in revenue. Accountants often must make financial recommendations to upper management and file necessary reports if the company is public.

Most accounting positions require a college education. Some may require the employee be a Certified Public Accountant. Experience as an accountant or CPA in the energy industry is usually required or considered a plus. Accountants must have a thorough knowledge of standard accounting procedures. They also need to be highly organized, pay attention to detail, and have excellent communication, math, and computer skills. If the company has a team of accountants and accounting clerks, there may be some employees reporting to the accountant. The average annual salary for accountants is between $40,000 and $90,000. Supervisory and management positions may be available at larger companies. In large operations this career path could lead to executive positions, such as chief financial officer. In the United States, accountants that file reports to the government must have the certified public accountant designation. This is usually obtained through a state agency and requires a combination of education, experience, and taking and passing an exam.

Compliance Manager

The compliance manager works primarily for the oil and natural gas industry, in which there are many laws and regulations in force directing exploration, extraction, and transmission of these products. This is because spills or leaks of oil or natural gas can have severe impacts on the environment and human health. Compliance managers must ensure that all regulations and guidelines are being followed at each operation.

To become a compliance manager, employees will first need to possess a bachelor's degree in science or technology. He or she will then need to work as a trainee, if a formal training program exists, or as an equipment operator, learning all aspects of the operation. Compliance managers must be able to work independently, although at times they will also work as part of a team. They should also have good communication and time management skills. Compliance managers will not have direct reports unless promoted to a supervisory or plant management position.

The average annual salary range for compliance managers is between $35,000 and $60,000, with trainees earning the lowest salaries. Once compliance managers have completed a trainee program or worked as an operator for a period of time, they will work independently as a compliance manager. From there it is possible for them to become supervisors or plant managers, or to advance their careers as independent consultants. Some states may require that compliance managers be certified.

Computer Software Engineer

Software engineers work in most industries, but can find many job opportunities in the energy industry. Software engineers are computer programmers that work with a company to determine their software needs and create custom software to meet them. The software could be to automate processes in the production end of the business, or the business/customer service end. Most software engineers will need to have a bachelor's degree in computer science, computer information systems, or software engineering. Depending on the type of programming required, a master's degree may be needed. Computer software engineers will need to have excellent analytical and problem solving skills. They also need to be innovative and creative, detail oriented, and able to multitask. In some large companies, if there are several programmers, the software engineer could have technicians or other employees who report to him or her.

The average annual salary for computer software engineers is approximately $85,000. The typical career path for software engineers employed by larger businesses includes promotions to project manager, manager of information systems, or even chief information officer. Computer software engineers can become certified to use specific computer program languages or tools.

Customer Service Representative

The customer service representative (CSR) is often employed by electric and or gas utility companies, although other energy producers hire them as well. Usually these employees answer questions and concerns that customers have about their bills and or energy usage. The customer service representative also works with the customer if he or she needs to make payment arrangements on his or her bill. Customer service representatives need to have a high school diploma, although some utility companies are now looking for employees who have an associate's degree in business or a related field. The most important skills needed by the CSR are good listening skills, good communication skills, and a desire to help the customer. Additionally, CSRs should have a sound understanding of the utility business, including how a customer's bill is calculated and what appliances and equipment in a home or business uses the most energy.

The average hourly wage for CSRs is between $13 and $18. After working as a CSR for several years, there is potential to be promoted to supervisor, although with this usually comes the expectation to earn a bachelor's degree. After becoming a supervisor, the person can be promoted to customer service manager of a large department. Certification is not required to get a CSR position, but there are different organizations that do offer certification for CSRs in various industries. Acquiring certification could give the CSR a competitive advantage if he or she is looking for a new job or promotion.

Customer Service Supervisor/Manager

Once a customer service representative has worked as a rep for a number of years, he or she may be promoted to customer service supervisor or manager. In this position, he or she will be responsible for ensuring that the reps he or she is supervising are giving customers quality customer service and working efficiently and effectively. They are also responsible for making sure that employees are well trained and have the tools and information they need to do a good job. Most employers hire supervisors and managers that have a bachelor's degree in business, communications, or other related field. Some managers or higher-level positions may require a master's degree in business administration.

Customer service supervisors or managers need to have very good people skills and communication skills. They should also have good conflict resolution skills, be able to motivate employees to do their best, and have excellent organizational and time management skills. Supervisors and managers have customer service representatives reporting to them. The average annual salary for customer service supervisors and managers is approximately $45,000. Customer service supervisors or managers may become higher-level managers at the corporate headquarters of the utility company. Certification is not required to get a CSR supervisor or manager position, but there are different organizations that do offer certification for CSR supervisors and managers in various industries. Acquiring certification could give the manager or supervisor a competitive advantage if he or she is looking for a new job or promotion.

Energy Consultant

The demand for energy consultants is increasing rapidly because they can result in new customers for different energy companies. While mostly employed by renewal energy segments of the industry, the energy consultant is also finding employment at more traditional energy employers who are discovering their value. The energy consultant works with large businesses, factories, and other customers to look at their energy usage and suggest ways for them to be more efficient, reduce their energy consumption, and ultimately save them money. Many large businesses and governments are also looking for ways to reduce their carbon emissions, and energy consultants can help with that as well.

Energy consultants will need to have a bachelor's degree in a type of engineering, such as electrical, mechanical or civil engineering. More colleges are developing specific programs and majors for energy consultants. Energy consultants need to have excellent analytical, problem solving, and decision-making skills. They should also have excellent communication and presentation skills, and be creative and innovative. In some large companies, the energy consultant may have an administrative person who reports to him or her, or if he or she becomes a manager or supervisor he or she will have direct reports.

The average annual salary for energy consultants $40,000 and $90,000, and could be higher, depending on whether they receive any bonuses or commission for products the clients purchase at his or her recommendation. In larger organizations, the energy consultant can become a supervisor or manager. He or she may also be able to advance his or her career by becoming an independent consultant or working for a government agency. Currently various organizations offer certification for energy consultants. People interested in this position should ask employers which certifications are considered the most reputable and important for the job.

Marketing Representative/Supervisor/Director

Marketing department personnel are responsible for successfully marketing a business or product of the business. This is also true for the energy industry. Marketing campaigns must meet budget requirements. Personnel will develop marketing material and choose appropriate advertising and promotional outlets. Depending on the segment of the industry, marketing personnel may also sell the company's products and services.

A college degree in business with an emphasis on marketing is a foremost requirement. Higher-level positions may require an MBA degree, as well as advertising agency experience or extensive knowledge of marketing strategies, techniques, and channels. Lower-level positions may require at least one to two years of previous industry experience. Marketing personnel should be highly creative, innovative, and have excellent communication skills, both written and spoken. They should also have good time management and project management skills.

The average annual salary for marketing department personnel is between $40,000 and $140,000, depending on the position and location. Marketing staff members start out as assistants or administrative personnel and become supervisors or managers. In some large companies, marketing personnel can eventually become executives. Certifications are not required to obtain employment, but are available through the American Marketing Association at Marketingpower.com.

Market Research Analyst

The market research analyst works in the marketing department, but performs a specific function that is unique. The research analyst is required to conduct research, take surveys, and gather as much data as possible about a specific market the company is interested in pursuing. This could mean the demographics and income levels of the market, as well as their preferences and needs for certain products.

A bachelor's degree and master's degree are both required for this position, usually in economics or marketing. Some positions require a doctoral degree. Research analysts must have highly developed analytical thinking skills. They also need to be creative, innovative, and have excellent communication skills. The analyst must have good computer skills as well as data analysis abilities. Higher-level positions may have administrative employees that report to him or her.

The average annual salary for market research analysts is $67,000. Market research analysts can advance their careers by being promoted to the position of marketing manager or a senior management position. He or she could also start his or her own consulting business. Certification is not required to obtain a job, but it can give a candidate a competitive edge over other candidates. Certification can be obtained through the Market Research Association at Mra-net.org.

Public Relations

This area of employment is typically found at the corporate level of the energy company. A public relations employee will be responsible for writing or editing written communications for both internal and external audiences, such as company newsletters and news releases.

This department may be responsible for interacting with the media or reviewing marketing and advertising material. A college degree in a related field, such as communications or journalism, is required. Public relations professionals must have excellent communication skills, including writing and public speaking skills. Some companies require previous experience, depending on the level of the position. Some positions may require event planning or project management skills or background. If the company and department are large, the public relations person could become manager of the department. Otherwise, there are usually no direct reports for this position.

The average annual salary for public relations personnel is between $40,000 and $90,000, and could be higher or lower, depending on the position and location. For example, larger metropolitan areas typically pay higher salaries than companies located in rural areas. In larger companies public relations department team members may be promoted to supervisory or management positions. Executive positions may also be available. Certifications or accreditation are not required to obtain employment, but are available through the Public Relations Society of America at Prsa.org.

Chapter 4

Tips for Success

No matter what segment of the energy industry you choose to work in or what job, working in the energy industry can mean hard physical labor, challenging projects, and developing new skills and knowledge. Since researchers in all of the major segments—electric, wind, solar, oil, and nuclear—are continually looking for ways to improve efficiency and delivery to customers, new methods and technologies are continually being introduced and tested. When they work, it can mean a lot of work for every employee in the energy company as they prepare to roll it out, from the workers generating electricity to the customer service representatives who will have to explain it to customers. Every worker can be impacted, and just as they learn this new system, another change is introduced.

This chapter will provide some tips for finding a job, creating a career path, building a solid professional reputation, and increasing your chances to receive a promotion. While many of these tips could apply to any industry, they are especially important in the energy industry, in which a solid reputation among coworkers, supervisors, and managers could mean the difference between a promotion or plodding along in the same job for 15 years.

Energy Employment: An Overview

There are many different kinds of jobs in the energy industry, as evidenced in the previous chapter. One thing that should be clear after reading through the listings of jobs is that in the energy industry there is a clear division between two types of jobs: outdoor positions and indoor positions. Typically, outdoor positions are those that require physical strength and abilities, while indoor positions are administrative, engineering, or customer-focused. In many energy companies these two divisions also carry the distinction of being staffed either by union or non-union workers, with the outdoor workers being part of the union and non-union workers the administrative, engineering, supervisory, and management employees. This creates a very different environment than in companies in which there are no unionized workers. It is very important for union workers and non-union workers to create a work environment in which each group is treated with mutual respect. After all, it takes all of the workers to make an energy company a success; no one job or set of jobs is more important than another in the energy industry.

Another aspect of the energy industry that just about all employees need to keep in mind is that there is a good possibility that at least once in their careers (and most likely many more times than that) they will need to work during a power outage. While outages are most often associated with electrical lines, other forms of power can also be impacted by floods, hurricanes, and other acts of nature and weather. When there are hundreds and thousands of customers without power, it is up to the power provider to restore service as soon as possible. For outdoor crews this can mean working in less than desirable weather conditions and very long shifts throughout the day and night. Union workers can be assured that they will not have to work more hours than the number specified as maximum in their labor contracts. They are also usually entitled to special pay and rest hours following an event like this. However, during hot summer months when thunderstorms can produce dangerous lightning and take out service to customers, they can end up working many hours of overtime.

Outdoor crews are not the only employees that work during outages. During an outage it is possible for the power company to receive thousands of phone calls from customers reporting their power being out and asking when it will be restored. They want to know how long the food in their refrigerators will stay good or have questions about their pets. Most customer service representatives are trained to answer the most common questions customers can ask during an outage. If a customer is identified as being on life support, he or she is given priority service. It can take a full staff of customer service representatives plus their supervisors and managers to handle these calls during the outage period. Engineers and engineering techs may also be working, inspecting the problem areas, and engineering designs to reconstruct services that may need it. Like the outdoor crews, customer service representatives, supervisors, managers, and engineers can work round the clock to provide service and answer questions during a power outage. Supervisors and managers are also the ones who create the most efficient plan for restoring service, keep track of the crews and their progress, and direct their efforts in the field. They also make sure staffing levels are adequate for the tasks at hand and order food, accommodations, or other supplies they might need. Some power crews are called in from neighboring towns and states, and accommodations must be found for them.

Fortunately, most outages are of a short duration. Partly in response to the major outage that occurred and crippled the northeast United States in 2003, the U.S. congress created an energy bill that passed in 2005. Donald Gilligan, president of the National Association of Energy Service Companies, says one part of that bill stipulates that energy companies must develop reliability standards, record keeping, audits, and cost investments. "If you violate this bill you could be charged a fine of up to $1 million per day," says Gilligan. While energy companies always took reliability seriously, they have since taken measures—like new methods of communication described in an earlier chapter of this book—to be alerted to customer outages sooner and restore them as soon as possible.

If employees are not working outside or providing customer service or performing administrative services inside, then they are probably engineers or researchers who have the challenging but exciting task of improving current generation or transmission infrastructure, including power delivery or metering systems, or creating new energy products. The ultimate goal is to provide customers with power at an affordable price, while minimizing the company's financial risks and resources. It is a challenging task that many find rewarding as well.

All in all, working in the energy industry is not for someone who is not drawn to the idea of providing service to customers and working hard to keep that service going. While many customers currently have no choice when it comes to choosing a power provider, it is very likely that status will change in the future, making it even more important for employees to provide their customers with the best service possible.

Getting a Job

Not long ago the primary method people used to get a job was to scour the want ads in newspapers. Then publications dedicated to job ads and advice for obtaining employment came along, adding another tool to the job search toolbox. But the tool that has truly revolutionized how people look for jobs is the Internet. Today, while employers still list openings in newspapers, the majority of employers and job seekers use various job boards and Web sites found on the Internet. Most employers post openings on one or several sites, which can then be re-posted at other sites. If a job seeker does not have Internet access at home, it is a good idea to go to the library at least a few times a week to check for new job postings. Many human resource professionals say in order to get a job, people today MUST use the Internet.

There are the major job Web sites like Monster.com, and Hotjobs. com, and there are also sites specific to the energy industry that post jobs. Most companies also post job openings on their Web sites. Most job recruiters in the energy industry and outside of the industry agree; job seekers need to use all of the resources available to them, and that means searching job boards as well as company Web sites.

Some of the most frequently visited job Web sites today are Yahoo! HotJobs, JobCentral.com, CollegeRecruiter, CareerBuilder, Monster.com, Job.com, Career.com, TrueCareers.com, Indeed.com, Net-Temps.com, and Craig's List. There are also several job board sites that list jobs exclusively for the energy industry or a specific segment of it. Here is a list of some of the more prominent job boards:

Drilling Site.com: This is a job board for the petroleum industry located at http://www.drillingsite.com.

Energy Central Jobs.com: A Web site that lists jobs in all segments of the industry located at http://www.energycentraljobs .com/employer.

Energy Jobs Network: This site is part of the National Society of Professional Engineers Web site and is found at http:// www.energyjobsnetwork.com.

Careers in Wind: This site lists jobs in the win energy segment and can be found at http://www.careersinwind.com.

My Green Scene.com: A site for renewable energy jobs found at http://www.mygreenscene.com.

Wind Industry Jobs.com: This site lists jobs in the wind energy industry worldwide. It is found at http://www.wind industryjobs.com.

Another great resource for finding jobs is through industry associations. Members of an association can check the association's Web site. Chances are that jobs are posted somewhere on the site, and there could be advantages to looking for jobs through an association. Often association job boards are only open to members, and the jobs posted may not be listed at traditional job boards, so the competition for these jobs can be much less intense.

Job seekers should keep in mind that Web sites are not the best way to obtain *every* job. HR managers say that as an employee migrates up the hierarchy into management he or she should understand the company culture and how to obtain such a position. Some companies offer only internal promotion while others may use third-party recruiting agencies to fill these management positions. The most effective way to know the answer to this is to check with the company first-hand.

Finally, many people find open positions through the old-fashioned word of mouth method. In other words, just ask. If you have a friend that works at the company you are interested in, give him or her a call and ask if there are any openings. Even if there are not openings at the time of your call, you have planted a seed in your friend's mind. When an opening pops up your friend may think of you. If the company you are interested in does not post job openings online, then it is also OK to call the human resources department and ask if there are any.

Networking

Many experts agree that networking is the best way to find a job in today's tough economy. Companies are flooded with résumés for every position they advertise. Networking is a way to stand out from the crowd, which is extremely important. Recruiters recommend reaching out to someone you have worked with—a boss, former employee, or colleague. Recruiters say not to mention that you are looking for a new job, only exploring new opportunities.

One of the biggest reasons networking is an effective way to land a job is that in general, hiring managers have a certain comfort level in really knowing a candidate—beyond what they learn during an interview—and personal referrals can go a long way in increasing a person's chances of getting a job. Do not forget that networking is not just accomplished through traditional means and relationships. Job seekers can also network through social Web sites such as Facebook, Twitter, and LinkedIn. As they network and interests broaden, they will find others with the same interests and connections to more people in the industry. New opportunities may come their way when they are not even looking for them.

Jon Hoffman, a human resources professional with the Holland Board of Public Works, the public utility company for Holland, Michigan, provided his input and views for this chapter. Hoffman says that before you start your job search you should know exactly what kind of job in the energy industry you are interested in. He recommends taking a number of steps to make this determination.

First of all, job seekers need to decide what they really like doing. If they like physical, outdoor labor, then they are probably going to be most interested in positions such as utility line worker, electric meter technician, or even underground service locator. If they like a mix of indoor and outdoor, then they might be more interested in an engineering-type job, such as substation technician or construction inspector. If job seekers prefer physical labor indoors, they should consider maintenance work at power plants. There are few other jobs that are involved in coal-fired power plants and nuclear power plants that involve the maintenance or control of large-size pumps, fans, conveyors, and pulverizers. These plants still generate about half of the electricity in the United States, and will do so for many decades to come.

Another step in the process of deciding what job you are interested in is thinking about whether you want to travel a lot or not. According to Hoffman, some specialized utility jobs involve quite a bit of travel. For example, boilermakers are specialized utility mechanics that fabricate and repair boiler tubes and pressure vessels. They have very technical training on welding metal to withstand extremely high pressures. They also travel a lot and are gone for extended periods of time. For the most part though, employees of an electric utility will be less likely to travel as a routine part of their jobs. The primary exception to this general rule is the employee who works for a utility contractor, a company that utilities hire to do work for them. This employee is more likely to travel as a regular part of the job.

Best
Practice

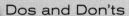

Dos and Don'ts

Dr. Randall S. Hansen is founder of Quintessential Careers, one of the oldest and most comprehensive career development sites on the Internet. He is also CEO of EmpoweringSites.com. He has put together a list of dos and don'ts when it comes to job interviews. While some of these may seem like common sense, you would be surprised how many people make these faux pas.

The dos:

- Do brush your teeth or pop a breath mint before the interview.
- Do travel to the interview location prior to the day of the interview so you are familiar with how to get there and how long it takes to do so.
- Do stress your accomplishments and dress appropriately.
- Do shake hands firmly, wait until you are asked to be seated, and avoid using poor language and pause words such as "um" and "uh."
- Do ask intelligent questions about the company and at the end of the interview tell the interviewer you want the job and ask about the next step in the process.

The don'ts:

- Don't chew gum during the interview.
- Don't bring up controversial topics.
- Don't speak negatively of previous bosses, companies, or co-workers.
- Don't smoke even if the interviewer does and offers you a cigarette.
- Don't tell jokes during the interview, and don't appear desperate for the job.
- Don't answer any question with a single yes or no answer. Instead give an explanation for your answer as much as possible.

Job seekers may find that one great place to go for information on various jobs in the energy industry is the U.S. Department of Labor's occupational web site, found at Onetonline.org. At this site, people can research different utility job families. To look at these families browse using the word "industry", and then by the word "utilities". The result is a list of high growth job titles in the field.

Whether electricity is generated through traditional methods, or through the use of solar, wind, or nuclear generating systems, typical career paths fall into three specific areas: (1) power generation (the making of electricity); (2) power transmission and distribution (moving power from the generation source to where it will be used); and (3) customer service and billing (measuring customer usage and billing them for it). The newest family of energy jobs that is still being developed and that are described on the site are the green energy jobs, which involve the alternative energy sources like wind and solar, and jobs that involve helping customers identify energy conservation opportunities.

Comparing and Matching Skills

Job seekers should also think about their current skills and abilities and compare them with the skills needed for the positions. Most jobs across all energy sources require solid basic math skills, good mechanical aptitude, and good observation skills (being able to inspect things visually and spot problems). Customer service and conservation jobs also require good people skills.

One important aspect to keep in mind is that many jobs in power generation and electric transmission and distribution require that the employee be able to handle working around heights. Power plants are multiple stories tall, and often require employees to walk on walkways that are made of metal grating, allowing them to look down to the floor far below. Most utility line workers still have to climb utility poles, and all of them need to be able to work comfortably from the bucket of a utility truck. New jobs in the wind turbine industry require even more tolerance of heights, as these turbines are up to 300 feet tall at the hub. Solar panels are often installed on roofs of multistory buildings. So, tolerance of heights is an important consideration if the person is considering an outdoor position in the industry.

Another skill needed in the energy industry is a high level of attention to detail. Many jobs in the industry involve working around power lines and substations. Because customers do not want to be without electricity, a lot of maintenance is done on energized equipment (equipment that is still "plugged in") by trained utility professionals who use special safety gear. When dealing with electricity, mistakes can be fatal. Individuals who are "afraid" of electricity probably should not consider jobs as utility line workers or substation technicians. Being respectful of electricity is the right approach; being afraid of it is not.

One of the biggest mistakes Hoffman sees people make is that they do not do the research and take the time to really think about what job is best for them. "I really believe that people leave way too much up to chance when it comes to choosing a job," he says. "In my experience, the average longevity of a current utility employee is between 10 and 14 years. If you figure about 2,000 hours of work per year, that means the decision to hire on to a utility ends up being a 20,000 to 28,000 hour commitment! It shouldn't be made lightly. The last thing anyone wants, employer or employee, is someone taking a job that they end up being miserable in."

Instead, job seekers should start with the big questions: Does the person want to work with his or her hands and body, or with his or her mind? Does he or she want to work indoors or outdoors? Does he or she want to do it him or herself or coordinate or supervise the work of others? Does he or she want to work directly with customers or primarily with other utility employees? Once these questions have been answered, the person can rule out the obvious misfits. For example, if the job seeker likes making people happy, then he or she probably does not want to be a collection worker, handling utility disconnects for non-payment. If the job seeker is afraid of heights or of electricity, then he or she probably does not want to be a utility line worker.

After the job seeker has narrowed down his or her list of jobs, it is time to look for the right kind of organization to work for. In the electric utility segment of the energy industry, investor-owned utilities are the companies usually thought of. Most of them are members of the Edison Electric Institute (EEI). Job seekers can check out EEI and its members online at Eei.org. Looking at the site's service territory map will give the potential employee an idea of what utility serves what locations in the country. Most large companies, big investor-owned utilities generally offer higher compensation than small utilities. They may also offer faster career growth opportunities. As with any large company, though, it is more likely that promotions will require relocation, and some jobs may involve more travel.

Options for Employment

Remember that in the electric utility industry there are also city (municipal) utilities and rural electric cooperatives. The rural electric cooperatives are like the utility industry's equivalent of credit unions. They are owned by their members. The National Rural Electric Cooperative Association Web (http://www.nreca.org) site provides a lot of information about these companies. There are also about 2,000 city-owned electric utilities in the United States. At one time these communities decided to create their own electric utility companies. The American Public Power Association Web site offers information about these companies and can be found at Publicpower.org. Most cooperative and municipal utilities are quite small. Their employees enjoy reasonably stable employment and the jobs do not require much travel. However, because these utilities are smaller, advancement opportunities may come along less frequently. One thing to note is that some cooperative or municipal utilities may have an unwritten hiring preference for individuals who are already living in their community. If the job seeker is already living in one of these communities, it could give them an edge on the competition.

Other employers in the electric utility industry are contractors. Most electric utilities contract out their utility line clearance (tree-trimming) services, and their directional underground construction work. Many electric utilities also contract out complex power plant work, including boiler and turbine inspections and repairs. One web site that lists a large number of current job openings with utility contractors is the National Utility and Excavation Contractors Association job board, which can be found at http://nuca.construction-jobs.com/nucacareercenter/home.cfm.

To learn more about employers in the other segments of the energy industry, such as solar, wind, nuclear, and petroleum, each has its own association (listings of these associations can be found in Chapter 6). Going to the association's Web site will allow the job seeker to browse their directory of members and become more familiar with the leading companies in each industry segment.

Obtaining an Internship

Another way for a person to test if he or she is right for a particular job can be obtaining an internship. While most internships are offered to students, a growing number of adults seeking second or third careers are also taking advantage of them. To find an internship, contact the local office of the investor-owned utility, municipal utility, co-op, or other energy company to see if it has an internship program. If it does not, Hoffman says it is OK to put together a proposal for the company to see if it will consider trying a pilot internship program. Of course the person proposing the program will serve as the first intern. He says the best selling point is that it is the cheapest labor the company can get, and the intern could end up being hired down the road once the person graduates or at the end of the internship. Hoffman recommends visiting the web site of The Society for Human Resource Management (http://www.shrm.org), which offers an excellent guide to organizing an internship program.

Even if an internship is not in the offing, job seekers can still learn more about the energy company and jobs at the company by talking to people who currently work there. Look at the jobs available on the company's Web site and call the company. Ask to meet with someone from HR. If an HR representative is too busy to meet, offer to take the representative out for lunch. It is a pretty rare person who will not make time for a free lunch, particularly if the job seeker is pleasant about asking. The $25 investment in the meal may be well worth spending after the person learns about the utility and its jobs. This is a good opportunity to find out how the utility fills vacancies. Some utilities still post opportunities internally first. If that is the case, job seekers may have to accept an entry-level position in the utility in order to eventually get the job they really want. If the position is unionized, make sure to understand the extent to which the utility is required to use seniority in making promotions. No one would want to hire on at a company only to find out that because he or she is the newest employee, it will be a decade before he or she has a shot at the position he or she is really interested in.

Landing the Position: Interview Tips

Once job seekers have determined what jobs they are most interested in and have used all of the resources available to find those jobs and applied to them, it is only a matter of time before they will be invited to interview for a position. In fact, Meg Matt, president and CEO of the Association of Energy Services Professionals, says that with the current shortage of workers people are surprised to hear they are likely to get a call for an interview very quickly. Just because an applicant is invited to an interview, however, does not mean he or she has the job in the bag. There are interviewing techniques, methods, dos and don'ts that can mean the difference between getting hired and getting passed by.

First, it is always the best policy for the interviewee to be honest about his or her goals, objectives, skills, and salary requirements. Like any good relationship, the job seeker is bound to end up mismatched with a job or company if he or she is not honest about what he or she is looking for. Many employers in the energy industry use panel interviews in which someone from human resources sits in the interview along with a manager, a supervisor, and maybe even a co-worker of the vacant position. When the interview is being set up, it is a good idea to ask to be given the names and titles of all of the participants. Having that information gives the interviewee a good idea of what to expect. The interviewee should also take extra copies of his or her résumé and cover letter to the interview, because it is possible that participants will not have received copies in advance.

Be prepared for some off-the-wall questions. There are new and popular interviewing techniques that are designed to give the interviewer an idea of your personality and characteristics. If you cannot think of an answer to any question it's OK to just say, "You know, I've never really thought about that before." Do not be afraid to be honest. If the interviewee is asked about his or her biggest mistake, he or she should tell them about it, and then tell them what he or she did to make things right.

Another general rule of them is not to focus on wages and benefits in the first interview. That discussion should be saved for later. However, if the job seeker really will not consider an offer that is below a certain range, this should be clarified when he or she is

Keeping in Touch

Electronic Etiquette

Jon Hoffman, human resources professional with the Holland Board of Public Works, Holland, Michigan, offers these tips for communicating electronically: Watch your electronic etiquette. Do not text while in meetings. Do not use text abbreviations in company e-mails. Do not forward chain mail jokes. Most importantly, if you need to have a frank discussion, do it face to face. It is much less likely to backfire than if you do it via e-mail.

contacted for the interview. At this point he or she can say, "I am very interested in working for your company and I am looking forward to our interview. I am also respectful of your time investment in considering me as a candidate. Would you be willing to share in general terms the compensation range for this position, so that I can confirm that our expectations overlap?"

Once the interviewee arrives at the interview, the first 30 seconds are important. Human resources professionals recommend that interviewees shake hands with the person or panel, look at the person or panel, and smile when introduced. If it is not clear where to sit, ask. If the interviewee is nervous, it is OK to admit it. It will help ease his or her tension, and may break the ice. Everyone at the interview has been in a job interview themselves, and they will understand. Human resources professionals also recommend bringing along written letters of reference, if they are available. If not, provide a list of references, preferably with e-mail addresses and phone numbers. Finally, do not forget to follow up the interview with a thank you e-mail *and* a written thank you note sent via U.S. mail.

A final note: If the company uses a particular set of skills assessments, job seekers can impress them by completing the assessments in advance of the interview. In some cases, the utility will require the completion of these assessments just to be considered for the position. Ask the person who phones to set up the interview if there are any assessments that need to be completed prior to the interview.

Building a Professional Reputation

Once you have obtained your dream job—or the closest thing to it—in the energy industry, the next thing you should be concerned about is building a professional reputation. Most human resource professionals advise employees to look at both their external customers and their internal customers when building a reputation. External customers are those outside of the company, and they do not just include customers, but those the employee does business with outside the company as well, such as bankers or contractors. That is why it is important for employees to conduct themselves professionally at all times.

Employees need to remember that a reputation is built on the person's actions and others' perceptions of those actions. One of the first places to start when building a professional reputation is with a professional image. The new employee should find out what is appropriate to wear in his or her job classification and in the company. Do engineers wear ties? Are blue jeans okay? What kind of footwear is appropriate? Remember, high heels will not work if the employee is driving around inspecting utility poles on back lot lines.

Next, communicate professionally. This is a key element of building a professional reputation. Employees should be friendly with those they encounter, but also to the point. Keep the majority of the communication work related. Stay away from debates on religion, politics, and racial and gender issues.

Another important way to build a positive professional reputation is to give credit where it is due. Nothing turns off co-workers faster than a "glory seeker" who never gives anyone else the credit for their work. The word will spread quickly, and the glory seeker will find himself or herself uninvited to project groups where the real action may be. This also means saying thank you to those who assist you with a project. A quick e-mail to that person thanking him or her for the assistance goes a long way toward building productive work relationships.

Respect is a very important factor in building a positive reputation. Since employees at many energy companies remain split into two basic groups: union (or labor) and non-union (or professional), the quickest way for a new employee to ruin his or her chances of success is to disrespect employees in the other group. Too often, union employees disrespect the roles of supervisors, managers, and other professionals (engineers, accountants, etc.) in the organization. The unionized workforce forgets that without the office people, customer bills would never get sent out, and paychecks would never get printed.

On the opposite side the same holds true: non-union college-educated professionals disrespect the experience and knowledge of frontline operators and utility fieldworkers. Professional employees can sometimes act as though having a four-year degree (or a two-year degree) makes them better humans than the frontline utility employees. This attitude shows, and can create hostility between frontline operators and professionals. Instead of starting a new position with this kind of attitude, the new employee should recognize that everyone at the company is proficient in something: Some people are proficient in engineering. Others are proficient in running power plants. Still others are proficient in trimming trees. It really does not matter if one person has three college degrees and another has a high school diploma. The new employee can learn something from each employee at the company.

Another great way to build a professional reputation is to get certified. Some larger companies often offer training and certification programs to their employees. There are a lot of specialty areas within the energy industry. Bulk power transmission and distribution is an engineering specialty. Utility fund accounting is an accounting specialty. Even human resources in a unionized utility environment is considered a specialty. Find out of there are utility-specific certification options related to the new position and pursue them. Once the new employee is certified, do what it takes to stay certified.

New employees can prevent the formation of a negative reputation by periodically asking others to review their work before it is submitted, especially if the employee is working on a particularly important project. It only makes sense to ask a coworker or someone in another department to review the calculations or final report before it is submitted. If the person finds no errors, thank them. If he or she does find an error, then that can be a good thing: it was caught before anyone else saw it.

Some human resources professionals recommend getting involved in a professional organization as a way to build a professional reputation outside the company. New employees can build an external network by going to seminars and conferences and if they participate in a unique project they can share their findings with their peers at these events. Seek to become the "go-to" person that others will think of when opportunities arise. New employees can become this person by learning as much as they can about the company and its operations. That does not mean they should forget their own core duties and responsibilities, but build relationships with employees in other departments and locations. This can make the employee invaluable to the company.

Establishing relationships with peers within the organization is easy to do when employees volunteer to participate in initiatives, committees, and other group activities. Even if the work seems unrelated to the person's job responsibilities, doing this builds on the employee's knowledge base and other employees will view the person positively.

How to Get Promoted

There is a school of thought that many professionals have that the way to earn a promotion is by obtaining that MBA. Others say the best way is to find a mentor within the organization who can offer advice and support. While neither of these methods is going to hurt anyone's chances of getting promoted, they should not be the only ones used. Sandy J. Wayne, professor and director of the Center for Human Resource Management at the University of Illinois, Chicago, conducted a study of 570 employees and 289 managers at a large company in the United States. She asked them to rank the most important factors influencing promotions. The results were surprising. What the employees thought would earn them promotions was very different than the factors cited by managers. As expected, having an MBA from a top school ranked at the top of the employees' list. Their bosses cited leadership skills as the most important factor. Employees also gave a high rank to having a mentor. Executives hardly mentioned this at all. They were looking for employees with a strong work ethic.

The fact is there is no magic bullet, formula, or method that will guarantee an employee a promotion. However, there are things workers can do to improve their chances and keep them top of mind so that when opportunities come up they will make the list of those considered. Human resource professionals agree that employees can forget any chances of promotion if they are not competent in their current position, which means they are meeting or exceeding their goals and objectives.

Once it is clear an employee has mastered his or her current position, there are actions that can be taken and things to avoid that will increase the chances of getting a promotion. One thing employees can do is look at the description of the job they want along with the skills it requires. It is highly likely that there will be skill sets that they either do not have, or have not been able to prove that they have. Managers are more likely to promote employees that take the initiative to acquire those skills that appear to be missing.

Many large companies offer training and development programs to fill in the gaps that an employee may have. If they do not offer their own training classes, they may reimburse employees for training they take on their own, especially if the class is related in some way to their current positions. For example, if the employee is a great marketing specialist but wants to be the manager of the marketing department he or she not only has to be a great marketing specialist, but also show that he or she can be a great leader. Employees can

INTERVIEW

The Future of Energy Careers

Meg Matt
President and CEO, Association of Energy Services Professionals,
Phoenix, Arizona

What jobs will be most in demand in the industry in the next several years?
Jobs that require special skills and education. On the production side of the business, the industry will see demand increase for line crews and engineers to keep the grid reliable and the power plants operating efficiently and safely. On the customer side of the meter, the industry will need engineers to design new customer programs, marketing gurus to promote them using standard and emerging communications channels, and market researchers and evaluators to interface with regulatory commissions and to ensure programs are meeting their goals.

What education or training will prove beneficial for new employees in the industry?
Electrical and mechanical engineers will be needed, as well those with advanced degrees in environmental and sustainability courses of study.

How are employers planning to attract quality candidates to the energy industry?
The energy industry needs to compete with other engineering-based organizations to attract the best and brightest talent entering the work force. Our association has created a foundation to help guide junior and high school students through the process of choosing colleges with specialized degrees via an interactive Web site. Organizations will need to commit to creating and sustaining challenging job assignments and programs for new employees to keep them engaged in the industry. Many organizations are developing long-term relationships with colleges, trade schools, and high schools to make sure students are aware of the many opportunities for challenging and interesting work in the energy industry.

accomplish this by showing the decision-makers they are willing to take on leadership assignments and prove they are willing to invest in themselves through training, reading, and education.

Problem
Solving

The Dilemma of Two Job Offers

It may not happen often, but the delightful dilemma of receiving two job offers does happen. Which one should the person choose? Unless the offers are nearly identical, and that is highly unlikely, there is a very good chance the employee is leaning toward one offer over the other. Of course there is also the situation when the person has received one offer and another one that may be more attractive is pending. Human resources managers say to be honest with the company that has already tendered the offer. The prospective employee should tell the company that he or she needs more time to contemplate the offer. Most companies will allow you up to a week to make the decision. However, if the company is pressed for time and needs an answer sooner it does not hurt for the prospective employee to let the person know that he or she is interviewing elsewhere. In fact, if the company that presented the offer knows that they may make their offer more attractive. It can certainly heighten a company's interest in the prospective employee. However, it is never a good idea to lie about it, if that is not the case. Once the prospective employee decides which job he or she will accept, that person needs to make sure he or she is gracious when declining the other offer. HR professionals say it is important to give a reason for the decision. The hiring manager or recruiter may not want to hear it, but the prospective employee owes it to them to explain why he or she made that decision.

Employees should pay close attention to what kind of experience and education is required for the position they are eying. If the employee has a high school education and the position requires an associate's degree, then start working on that associate's degree. If the position comes open before the employee has finished his or her degree, the person should apply anyway, and explain in the cover letter how far he or she has come toward the degree and the excellent grades the person has earned.

Just as in building a good reputation, getting involved in other activities at the company is also a great method for eventually getting a promotion. When employees volunteer to help out, organize, and lead projects and community work they demonstrate to managers that they can supervise and lead others. Human resources professionals also recommend that employees work with their current supervisor to develop a strategy that will lead to the job they are eying. They can also find a mentor in the department they want to move into, letting the person know of their interest and asking him or her to mentor them. But remember not to rely on mentoring alone. Mentoring will only work if employees have proven themselves capable in their current position and are working to prove they have the skills required to move to the next level.

Every company has its own unique culture and method for promoting employees, and this is true in the energy industry. In *The Realities of Management Promotion: An Investigation of Factors Influencing the Promotion of Managers in Three Major Companies*, authors Marian N. Ruderman and Patricia J. Ohlott looked at 64 promotions that occurred at three Fortune 500 companies and asked what had led to them. One surprising find was that jobs were often created to fit the candidate. The decision-makers did not place much emphasis on formal assessments such as performance evaluations.

Ruderman and Ohlott also found that in almost half of the cases, only one person was considered for the job. Tremendous variety existed among the types of promotions. The bottom line of the research was that organizational context should be considered when trying to understand promotions. Employees must spend time to really understand the company's culture and the process used to hire and promote if they want to advance in that organization. Each company will be different; employees need to ask questions and do their homework.

Elizabeth Freedman, MBA, is an award-winning speaker and business columnist, and is the author of *Work 101: Learning the Ropes of the Workplace without Hanging Yourself,* and *The MBA Student's Job-Seeking Bible*. She offers some dos and don'ts when it comes to seeking promotions. Among her dos are: Employees should imitate the people who hold the job they are interested in. She advises people to take them out to coffee or lunch and ask questions about what qualities have made them successful on the job. She also advises employees to become an expert in their field. She encourages workers to join industry associations and groups and attend their meetings and seminars even if they have to pay for them on their own. She says that the education and networking they will experience will be worth every penny of the investment and make them more marketable to their company and others.

Another big DO on Freedman's list is for employees to understand their boss and his or her priorities. When employees see how their job fits in with their boss's and they prioritize their work in harmony with his or hers, they make the boss look good—and, in turn, the employee will look good. It will also help to distinguish the time to ask questions from the time when the boss needs to be left alone. According to Freedman, these kinds of considerations go a long way.

Another point she makes is that employees need to make an effort to get along with all coworkers no matter what their ages. This is especially true in the energy industry. Although most of the workforce is older, there will soon be an influx of younger employees so the workforce can be anywhere from age 16 to 65. While people tend to gravitate toward people their own age, or think of younger people as their kids or older people as their parents, when working with people of different age ranges it is important to put those tendencies aside and find common ground. An energy company staff has to work together as a team if it is going to function smoothly and for all members to be successful. So in order to get promoted it is important to remember everyone is on the same team and try to get along.

There are also some pretty important "don'ts" on Freedman's list. One of her top don'ts is not to try to fight the current system. Even if employees clearly see some of its inefficiencies, the best way to correct them is working with the system rather than against it. Making suggestions for improvements is a positive way to initiate needed changes. Employees need to remember where they are in the hierarchy and work within the scope of their position as they try to make things more efficient.

Another sure way for employees to stifle their chances of promotion, according to Freedman, is to get the reputation as a complainer. The employee may be entirely correct about the problems within the organization, but if he or she takes every opportunity to complain about them rather than taking a more positive approach, the employee will be seen as the complainer instead of the person with great ideas for improvement. Freedman says the employee also runs the risk of being seen as someone who is not knowledgeable enough about the company or the industry to know what works and what does not. The best way to for employees to proceed when things just are not "right" in their eyes is to do their research, ask questions, and make suggestions to decision makers. Keep complaints private.

Lastly, do not become invisible, says Freedman. New employees may be overwhelmed with work, learning the company and the job, but if they bury themselves and do not volunteer to help others or make a real effort to connect with coworkers on a regular basis their name swill not be among the first mentioned when an opportunity comes along.

Pursuing Promotions: Polite and Persistent

Human resources professional Jon Hoffman says that when it comes to pursuing promotions, there is a fine line between being assertive and being obnoxious. The goal is to be the first, i.e. politely assertive, but not the second, obnoxious. One good way to for employees to start is by asking their supervisor or the human resources department if they can have a blank copy of the company's performance review form so that they will know in advance what they will be evaluated on. If their manager or supervisor does not schedule regular performance discussions, then the employee should take matters into his or her own hands. He or she can ask to meet with a supervisor after three months on the job, again after six months on the job, and again after one year on the job. He or she should let the supervisor know the meeting will take no more than one hour. Then he or she should use the hour to honestly express an appreciation for the job, share any disappointments or frustrations (in a professional manner, not whining!), discuss how their work has helped the department meet strategic goals, and propose an action plan for the next time period. At that time he or she should let their supervisor know that they are interested in progressing, and that they would like his/her advice on how to best prepare for opportunities within the company.

If after these meetings and preparations an employee gets bypassed for a promotion, it is best to approach the situation from a positive angle. The conversation can begin something like, "I really appreciate that you considered me for that vacancy. I imagine there were a number of people interested in it, and I am sure you had to weigh a lot of variables in making the choice that you did. Now that you've made your selection, I am wondering if you would be willing to give me any constructive feedback about how I could increase my odds of being selected if this opportunity comes open again." If the supervisor/manager is not comfortable having this discussion, set up a meeting with a representative of the human resources department and ask him or her.

Throughout the year, employees should keep a running list of significant projects and tasks that they have been part of or have completed. They may be surprised at how many of these projects there actually are. Then, when a promotional opportunity comes up, the employee can write a cover letter for his or her résumé that weaves in a number of these items. They should not overwhelm the letter. Instead they should just be dropped in as appropriate. Others in the organization may not have any idea what the employee has been working on, and it certainly will not hurt to let them know.

Work hard, and work smart. In most energy companies, employees really do not have to do a whole lot extra to stand out. Employees that are expected to maintain a specific work schedule need to stick to it. They need to arrive on time in the morning, not drag out lunch periods, and not always leave five minutes before the end of the day. (In the course of a year, that five minutes adds up to 20 hours.) Hoffman says that his experience has been that employees do not have to work 60-hour weeks in most utilities in order to be noticed. They may need to work 45 hours a week, with the occasional 50-hour workweek thrown in. He also recommends that employees use company-approved technology to help others in the company keep track of their whereabouts. If they are in meetings, make sure their shared Microsoft Outlook calendar is up to date. Nobody likes having to hunt someone else down in order to get an answer to an urgent question. Paying attention to these details is what leads to promotions.

Career Planning

Like getting a promotion, there is no one way or "right way" to plan a career in the energy industry or any other industry for that matter. Experts agree—employees must know what career path they really want, and then work with key people to develop a plan to get it. Identifying and developing this career path may be the easy part for some employees. For others it is not so easy. Freedman says there have been numerous cases of people spending years pursuing a specific career only to land that dream job and realize it was not what they thought it was at all. To prevent that situation from occurring, if they have not already done so, potential employees need to spend some time in the area of the industry they have chosen. They need to talk to people who are already where they want to be and ask them lots of questions. Make sure the career path they are choosing is really going to give them the end results they are looking for.

Career planning takes some self-awareness and initiative, as well as a lot of research, time, and effort. Once someone has decided what his or her career path looks like, the next step is to make sure those goals are realistic. Not everyone can be the CEO of a utility or energy company, but perhaps the director or vice president is a more within the person's grasp. Then, depending on the person's ultimate goal and where he or she happens to be now, the employee has a few options. If the person is employed by a larger company with a human resources department, human resources professionals recommend that the person meet with a professional in that department to discuss his or her career goals and develop a career plan. Human resources professionals can help employees develop a plan, but it is to remember that the individual person is still responsible and accountable for making it happen. The human resources department will not do that.

Then, just as they did when working toward a promotion, employees should look at the skills required for their ultimate goal and then at the skills they currently possess. If they are missing some basic skills they need to take it upon themselves to develop them, either through the company they work for and the training it has to offer, or through other educational opportunities like college courses and continuing education through industry associations. In a rapidly changing industry like the energy industry, it is essential for employees to continue to stay in touch with industry trends, company culture, and opportunities inside and outside their current scope of responsibilities. They will be much more likely to reach their ultimate goal and travel along their career paths in the manner they wish to.

Continuing Education and Certifications

Today just about every job in every industry offers continuing education and certifications, and the energy industry is no exception to that rule. As evidenced by the listing of jobs in Chapter 3, a great number of jobs in the energy industry are technical positions, and most of them either require certification or highly recommend it. Even of a job does not fit that description, certification does not hurt, and can give an employee a competitive edge over those who do not hold the certifications. Most engineering jobs require that the employee is a licensed professional engineer, so it is clear what licenses or certifications are required. Other technical positions, such as employees working in nuclear power plants, also must be certified or licensed by the state. There are a number of jobs, though, such as customer service professionals, for which the path for continuing education or certification is not clear-cut.

Generally speaking, most employees in the industry can get certifications related to their field through an industry association. For example, if the employee is a public relations coordinator for a solar energy company, he or she can get certification through the Public Relations Society of America. Certain professions, like IT professionals must be certified in certain software and management programs to land specific jobs. However, before employees take the time and spend the money to earn a certification, it is a good idea to talk to managers and HR professionals to make sure it will truly benefit them, either in their current position, or in a hoped-for future position.

Tess Price has a PhD in Human Resources Organizational Development and adult education and is a columnist for Office Arrow, a professional development Web site for administrators. Price says certifications can mean the difference in whether someone is considered or hired for a particular job. "If you are certified in your job area but another applicant is not, you may improve your chances of getting an interview or being hired," she states. In fact, she adds that it may actually be a satisfactory substitute for secondary education in some fields. But to determine whether certification and continuing education is needed, it is always best for employees to rely on a human resources professional and the culture in their company.

Chapter 5

Talk Like a Pro

The energy industry can be a highly technical one. Whether it is calculating transformer capacity or engineering a gas well, there is a great deal of science involved in many energy jobs. No matter what kind of job you choose to pursue, it will benefit you to know and understand some of the technical and even not-so-technical terms you might encounter.

In this chapter you will find an A-to-Z listing of some of the most prevalent industry terms and their meanings. Read through these pages and learn the ones that are most applicable to your career. Then keep this book handy as a future reference guide; you never know when someone will throw a "new" term your way.

above-market cost The cost of an energy service that is more than the cost of similar services in the energy market.

access charge A fee charged to an electric supplier or one of its primary customers for accessing a power company's transmission or distribution lines.

active solar A solar energy system in which energy from the sun is collected and stored using pumps or fans and a storage tank system.

adjustment bid When an independent energy system operator (ISO) adjusts a bid according to forecasted supply and demand.

adverse hydro Conditions that affect the ability to generate hydroelectricity; examples include low rainfall and snowfall amounts.

affiliated power producer A company that generates power and that is affiliated with a utility company.

after-market conversion The act of using a kit to convert a vehicle so that it operates on an alternative fuel.

AGA American Gas Association.

aggregator A broker (that sells energy), a company that markets, or a government entity that negotiates the purchase of electricity based on the combined loads of many end-users.

alcohol fuels Liquid chemicals that have specific combinations of hydrogen, carbon, and oxygen, and that are capable of being used as fuel.

alternating current (AC) Electric current that reverses its flow at regular periods of time. Almost all power produced by electric utilities in the United States shifts direction at a rate of 60 times per second.

alternative energy sources Sources of energy other than those (i.e., fossil fuels, nuclear, and hydropower) traditionally used.

alternative fuels a fuel cannot be labeled as an alternative fuel unless it fits the description that has been given in the National Energy Policy Act. This act says that alternative fuels must be contain between 70 percent and 85 percentmethanol, denatured ethanol, and other alcohols, separately or in mixtures with gasoline or other fuels. Other fuels that can achieve this label according to the act include coal-derived liquid fuels, fuels other than alcohols derived from biological materials, electricity, or any other fuel that is not primarily petroleum and that results in substantial energy savings and substantial reduction in the harm to the environment.

alternative fuel vehicle (AFV) A vehicle designed to operate on an alternative fuel or in combination with a traditional fuel (i.e., compressed natural gas, methane blend, electricity).

annual requirement The report that all companies that operate underground natural gas storage facilities are required to submit to the U.S. Department of Energy, providing their estimates of how much gas they used and will use in the current reporting year.

ANSI American National Standards Institute.

anthracite A type of coal used commonly for residential and commercial heating.

appliance saturation A percentage describing the proportion of all households in a given geographical or service area that have a certain appliance.

apparent consumption (coal)   The sum of domestic coal production, plus coal imports, minus coal exports.

apparent consumption (natural gas)   The sum of the nation's dry natural gas production, plus imports, minus exports.

apparent power   The product of the voltage (in volts) and the current (in amperes). It comprises both active and reactive power. It is measured in volt-amperes and often expressed in kilovolt-amperes (kVA) or megavolt-amperes (MVA).

API   The American Petroleum Institute, a trade association.

area load   A number that describes the total amount of electricity consumers in a specific utility's service territory are using.

associated gas   Natural gas that can be developed for commercial use, and which is found in contact with oil in naturally occurring underground formations.

Atomic Energy Commission   The independent civilian agency of the federal government formed to supervise and promote the use of nuclear energy. The agency's functions were taken over in 1974 by the Energy Research and Development Administration (now part of the U.S. Department of Energy) and the Nuclear Regulatory Commission.

auxiliary generator   A generator at an electric plant site that provides power for the actual operation of the electrical generating equipment.

balancing authority (electric)   An entity in a specific region that is responsible for ensuring there will be enough power generated to meet the region's electric demand. **balancing item** Represents the differences between the sum of the components of the natural gas supply and the sum of the components of the natural gas dispensed, usually due to quantities lost or the effects of data reporting problems.

base load   The lowest amount of power production a specific set of customers need during a season or year.

base load unit   A power-generating facility that is expected to operate at near-capacity levels as often as possible.

baseline forecast   A prediction of future energy needs that does not take into account the likely effects of new conservation programs.

base rate   The portion of the total electric or gas rate that covers the general costs of doing business unrelated to fuel expenses.

bi-fuel vehicle   A motor vehicle that operates on two different fuels, but not on a mixture of the fuels. Each fuel is stored in a separate tank.

Everyone
Knows

Units of Measure

Whether you work for a utility company or an oil production company, one of the things everyone will expect you to know are the units of measurements used in the industry. Here is a listing of some of the most common units of measure used in the energy industry.

Ampere (Amp): The unit of measurement that describes the amount of electrical current produced by a circuit or conductor.

British thermal unit (BTU): The standard measure of heat energy. It takes 1 Btu to raise the temperature of 1 lb of water by 1degree Fahrenheit at sea level.

Barrel: A unit of volume of fuel, usually oil, equal to 42 U.S. gallons.

Barrels per day equivalent (BPD-equivalent): A unit of measure that tells how much oil would have to be burned to produce the same amount of energy. For example, California's hydroelectric generation in 1983 was 58,000 barrels per day equivalent.

Footcandle: A unit of illuminance on a surface that is one foot from a uniform point source of light of one candle and is equal to one lumen per square foot.

Gigawatt (GW): One thousand megawatts (1,000 MW) or, one million kilowatts (1,000,000 kW) or one billion watts (1,000,000,000 watts) of electricity.

Gigawatt-hour (GWH): One million kilowatt-hours of electric power.

Horsepower (HP): A unit for measuring the rate of doing work. One horsepower equals about three-fourths of a kilowatt (745.7 watts).

bioconversion Processes that use plants or microorganisms to change one form of energy into another. For example, an experimental process uses algae to convert solar energy into gas that could be used for fuel.

biodiesel A biodegradable transportation fuel for use in diesel engines that is produced through the transesterification (conversion of one type of ester into another) of organically-derived oils or fats. It may be used either as a replacement for or as a component of diesel fuel.

kBtu: One thousand (1,000) Btus.

Kilovolt (kv): One thousand volts (1,000).

Kilowatt (kW): One thousand (1,000) watts.

Kilowatt-hour (kWh): The most commonly used unit of measure telling the amount of electricity consumed over time. It means one kilowatt of electricity supplied for one hour.

Lumen: A measure of the amount of light available from a light source equivalent to the light emitted by one candle.

Lumens/watt: A measure of the efficacy of a light fixture; the number of lumens output per watt of power consumed.

MCF: One thousand cubic feet of natural gas, having an energy value of one million Btu. A typical home might use six MCF in a month.

Megawatt (MW): One thousand kilowatts (1,000 kW) or one million (1,000,000) watts.

Megawatt-hour (MWh): One thousand kilowatt-hours, or an amount of electrical energy that would supply 1,370 typical homes in the Western U.S. for one month.

Therm: One hundred thousand (100,000) British thermal units (1 therm = 100,000 Btu).

Volt: A unit of electromotive force required to drive a steady current of one ampere through a resistance of one ohm. Electrical systems of most homes and offices have 120 volts.

Watt: A unit of measure of electric power at a point in time, as capacity or demand. One watt of power maintained over time is equal to one joule per second.

Watt-hour: One watt of power expended for one hour.

biomass   Energy resources derived from organic matter, including wood, agricultural waste, and other living-cell material that can be burned to produce heat energy. Resources also include algae, sewage, and other organic substances that may be used to make energy through chemical processes.

blackout   A power loss affecting many electricity consumers over a large geographical area for a significant period of time.

bottled gas   The liquefied petroleum gases propane and butane, contained under moderate pressure (about 125 pounds per square inch and 30 pounds per square inch respectively), in cylinders.

bottoming cycle The heat produced by a steam-electric generating system that is not used in the system, and the subsequent reintroduction of this heat into the system to increase efficiency.

breeder reactor A reactor that both produces and consumes fissionable fuel, especially one that creates more fuel than it consumes. The new fissionable material is created by a process known as breeding, in which neutrons from fission are captured in fertile materials.

brownout A controlled power reduction in which the utility decreases the voltage on the power lines so customers receive weaker electric current. Brownouts can be used if total power demand exceeds the maximum available supply. The typical household does not notice the difference.

busbar A section of aluminum or copper designed to conduct electricity and that is used in distribution systems.

buy through An agreement between utility and customer to import power when the customer's service would otherwise be interrupted.

buyer An entity that purchases electrical energy or services from the power exchange (PX) or through a bilateral contract on behalf of end-use customers.

call-back A provision included in some power sale contracts that lets the supplier stop delivery when the power is needed to meet other specific obligations.

capacity The amount of electric power for which a generating unit, generating station, or other electrical apparatus is rated either by the user or manufacturer. The term is also used for the total volume of natural gas that can flow through a pipeline over a given amount of time, considering such factors as compression and pipeline size.

capacity factor A percentage of a power plant's capacity that is used over time; it is calculated by taking the actual capacity of the plant during a specified time frame, and dividing it by the capacity that would've been achieved had the plant operated nonstop during that same time frame.

capacity release A secondary market for capacity that is contracted by a customer that is not using all of its capacity.

captive customer   A customer who does not have realistic alternatives to buying power from the local utility, even if that customer has the legal right to buy from competitors.

carbon dioxide (CO2)   A colorless, odorless, nonpoisonous gas that is a normal part of the Earth's atmosphere. Carbon dioxide is a product of fossil fuel combustion as well as other processes and is considered a greenhouse gas.

carbon monoxide (CO)   A colorless, odorless, highly poisonous gas made up of carbon and oxygen molecules formed by the incomplete combustion of carbon or carbonaceous material, including gasoline. It is a major air pollutant on the basis of weight.

carrying costs   Costs incurred in order to retain natural resource exploration and property rights at a specific location after its acquisition, but before production has occurred, including legal costs for title defense and delay rentals.

chlorofluorocarbon (CFC)   Any of various compounds consisting of a combination of carbon, hydrogen, chlorine, and flourine used as refrigerants. CFCs are now thought to be harmful to the Earth's atmosphere.

chemical energy   The energy generated when a chemical compound combusts, decomposes, or transforms to produce new compounds.

circuit   A complete run of a set of electric conductors from a power source to various electrical devices (appliances, lights, etc.) and back to the same power source.

clean fuel vehicle   A term that is frequently but incorrectly used interchangeably with "alternative fuel vehicle". Generally, refers to vehicles that use low-emission, clean-burning fuels.

climate change   A term used to refer to all forms of climatic inconsistency, but especially to significant change from one prevailing climatic condition to another. In some cases, "climate change" has been used synonymously with the term "global warming" although scientists tend to use the term in a wider sense, including natural changes in climate and climatic cooling.

coal   Black or brown rock, formed under pressure from organic fossils in prehistoric times, that is mined and burned to produce heat energy.

coal conversion   Changing coal into synthetic gas or liquid fuels. (*See* gasification.)

coal oil   Oil that can be obtained by distilling bituminous coal.

coal slurry pipeline   A pipe system that transports pulverized coal suspended in water.

cogeneration   The production of electrical energy and another form of useful energy like heat or steam.

coke   A residue high in carbon content and low in hydrogen that is the final product of heating coking coal to around 1000°C to 1100°C in the absence of oxygen.

combined cycle plant   An electric generating station that uses waste heat from its gas turbines to produce steam for conventional steam turbines.

combustion burning   Rapid oxidation (the addition of oxygen to a compound with a loss of electrons), with the release of energy in the form of heat and light.

comfort conditioning   The process of treating air to simultaneously control its temperature, humidity, cleanliness, and distribution to meet the comfort requirements of its occupants.

competitive transition charge   A non-bypassable charge levied on each customer of the distribution utility, including those who are served under contracts with nonutility suppliers, for recovery of the utility's stranded costs that develop because of competition.

commercialization   Programs or activities that increase the value or decrease the cost of integrating new products or services into the electricity sector.

compressed natural gas (CNG)   Natural gas that has been compressed under high pressure, typically between 2,000 and 3,600 pounds per square inch, and held in a container. The gas expands when released for use as a fuel.

condensate   Liquid fuel obtained by burning gas or vapor produced from oil and gas wells.

conductor   Metal wires, cables, and busbar used for carrying electric current. Conductors may be solid or stranded, that is, built up by an assembly of smaller solid conductors.

contingency planning   The U.S. Energy Commission's strategy to respond to impending energy emergencies such as a shortage of fuel or power because of natural disasters or the result of human or political causes, or those that pose a clear threat to public health, safety, or welfare. The contingency plan specifies actions to address the potential impacts of a possible shortage or disruption of petroleum, natural gas, or electricity.

contract price   The delivery price determined when a contract is signed. It can be a fixed price or a base price escalated according to a given formula.

convection   Transferring heat by moving air or transferring heat by means of upward motion of particles of liquid or gas heat from beneath.

conventional gasoline   Finished motor gasoline not included in the oxygenated or reformulated gasoline categories.

conversion   Device or kit by which a conventional fuel vehicle is changed to an alternative fuel vehicle.

converter   Any technology that changes the potential energy in a fuel into a different form of energy such as heat or motion. The term is also used to mean an apparatus that changes the quantity or quality of electrical energy.

cooling degree day   A unit of measure that indicates how heavy the air conditioning needs are under certain weather conditions.

cooperative electric utility   An electric utility legally established to be owned by and operated for the benefit of those using its service. Most electric cooperatives have been initially financed by the Rural Utilities Service (prior Rural Electrification Administration), U.S. Department of Agriculture.

corporate average fuel economy (CAFE)   A sales-weighted average fuel mileage calculation, in terms of miles per gallon, based on city and highway fuel economy measurements performed as part of the federal emissions test procedures.

crude oil   Petroleum as found in the Earth, before it is refined into oil products.

crude oil stocks   Stocks held at refineries and at pipeline terminals. Does not include stocks held on leases (storage facilities adjacent to the wells).

day-ahead market   The market for energy for the next day.

degree day   A unit, based upon temperature difference and time, used in estimating fuel consumption and specifying nominal annual heating load of a building. When the mean temperature is less than 65 degrees Fahrenheit, the heating degree days are equal to the total number of hours that temperature is less than 65 degrees Fahrenheit for an entire year.

delivered cost   The cost of fuel, including the invoice price of fuel, transportation charges, taxes, commissions, insurance, and expenses associated with leased or owned equipment used to transport the fuel.

demand   The rate at which energy is delivered to loads and scheduling points by generation, transmission, or distribution facilities.

demand side management (DSM)   The methods used to manage energy demand, including energy efficiency, load management, fuel substitution, and load building.

Department of Energy (DOE)   A department established by the United State government's Department of Energy Organization Act to consolidate the major federal energy functions into one cabinet-level department to formulate a comprehensive, balanced national energy policy.

dependable capacity   A power system's ability to carry the electric power for the time interval and period specified. Dependable capacity is determined by such factors as capability, operating power factor, and portion of the load the station is to supply.

depletable energy sources   Electricity purchased from a public utility; energy obtained from burning coal, oil, natural gas, or liquefied petroleum gases.

deregulation   The elimination of some or all regulations from a previously regulated industry or sector of an industry.

diesel oil   Fuel for diesel engines obtained from the distillation of petroleum.

diffuse radiation   Solar radiation scattered by water vapor, dust, and other particles as it passes through the atmosphere, so that it appears to come from the entire sky. Diffuse radiation is higher on hazy or overcast days than on clear days.

direct access   The ability of a retail customer to purchase commodity electricity directly from the wholesale market rather than through a local distribution utility.

direct current (DC)   Electricity that flows continuously in the same direction.

direct energy conversion   Production of electricity from an energy source without transferring the energy to a working fluid or steam. For example, photovoltaic cells transform light directly into electricity. Direct conversion systems have no moving parts and usually produce direct current.

direct radiation   Radiation that has traveled a straight path from the sun, as opposed to diffuse radiation.

direct solar gain   Solar energy collected from the sun (as heat) in a building through windows, walls, or skylights.

distributed generation   Small amounts of generation located on a utility's distribution system for the purpose of meeting local (substation level) peak loads and/or displacing the need to build additional (or upgrade) local distribution lines.

distribution   The delivery of electricity to the retail customer's home or business through low voltage distribution lines.

distribution system (electric utility)   The substations, transformers, and lines that convey electricity from high-power transmission lines to consumers.

distribution utility (DISCO)   The regulated electric utility entity that constructs and maintains the distribution wires connecting the transmission grid to the final customer. The DISCO can also perform other services such as aggregating customers, purchasing power supply and transmission services for customers, billing customers and reimbursing suppliers, and offering other regulated or non-regulated energy services to retail customers. The "wires" and "customer service" functions provided by a distribution utility could be split so that two totally separate entities are used to supply these two types of distribution services.

diversity   The electric utility system's load is made up of many individual loads that make demands upon the system, usually at different times of the day. The individual loads within the customer classes follow similar usage patterns, but these classes of service place different demands upon the facilities and the system grid.

diversity exchange   An exchange of capacity, energy, or both capacity and energy between systems whose peak loads occur at different times.

divestiture   The stripping off of one utility function from the others by selling (spinning-off) or in some other way changing the ownership of the assets related to that function.

downstream   A term used in the petroleum industry referring to the refining, transportation, and marketing side of the business.

dry bulb temperature   A measure of the sensible temperature of air.

dry hole   An exploratory or development well found to be incapable of producing either oil or gas in sufficient quantities to justify completion as an oil or gas well.

dry steam   The conventional type of geothermal energy used for electricity production in California. Dry steam captured at the

Earth's surface is used to run electric turbines. The principal dry steam resource area in the United States is The Geysers in Northern California.

dump energy   Energy generated in a hydroelectric plant by water that cannot be stored or conserved.

economic efficiency   A term that refers to the optimal production and consumption of goods and services. This generally occurs when prices of products and services reflect their marginal costs.

economies of scale   Cost advantages that a business obtains due to a construction project or capital improvement.

efficiency   The ratio of the useful energy delivered by a dynamic system (such as a machine, engine, or motor) to the energy supplied to it over the same period or cycle of operation. The ratio is usually determined under specific test conditions.

electric generator   A device that converts a heat, chemical, or mechanical energy into electricity.

electric radiant heating   A heating system in which electric resistance is used to produce heat, which radiates to nearby surfaces. There is no fan component to a radiant heating system.

electric resistance heater   A device that produces heat through electric resistance. For example, an electric current is run through a wire coil with a relatively high electric resistance, thereby converting the electric energy into heat that can be transferred into a space by fans.

electric utility   Any person or state agency with a monopoly franchise (including any municipality), which sells electric energy to end-use customers; this term includes the Tennessee Valley Authority, but does not include other federal power marketing agencies (from EPAct).

electrolysis   Breaking down a chemical compound into its elements by passing a direct current through it.

electromagnetic fields (EMF)   Magnetic and electric fields produced by ordinary use of electricity. These 60-hertz fields (fields that go back and forth 60 times a second) are associated with electrical appliances, power lines, and wiring in buildings.

embedded costs exceeding market prices (ECEMP)
Embedded costs of utility investments exceeding market prices are: 1) costs incurred pursuant to a regulatory or contractual obligation; 2) costs that are reflected in cost-based rates; and

3) cost-based rates that exceed the price of alternatives in the marketplace.

emergency core cooling system (ECCS)   Equipment designed to cool the core of a nuclear reactor in the event of a complete loss of the coolant.

emission standard   The maximum amount of a pollutant legally permitted to be discharged from a single source.

emissivity   The property of emitting radiation, possessed by all materials to a varying extent.

energy   The capacity for doing work. Forms of energy include: thermal, mechanical, electrical, and chemical. Energy may be transformed from one form into another.

energy budget   A requirement in the Building Energy Efficiency Standards that a proposed building be designed to consume no more than a specified number of Btus per year per square foot of conditioned floor area.

energy charge   The amount of money owed by an electric customer for kilowatt-hours consumed.

energy consumption   The amount of energy consumed in the form in which it is acquired by the user. The term excludes electrical generation and distribution losses.

energy (fuel) diversity   Policy that encourages the development of energy technologies to diversify energy supply sources, thus reducing reliance on conventional (petroleum) fuels.

energy efficiency   The practice of using less energy/electricity to perform the same function. Programs designed to use electricity more efficiently, doing the same with less.

energy efficiency ratio (EER)   The ratio of cooling capacity of an air conditioning unit in British thermal units (Btus) per hour to the total electrical input in watts under specified test conditions.

energy management system   A control system (often computerized) designed to regulate the energy consumption of a building by monitoring the operation of energy consuming systems such as heating, ventilation, and air conditioning.

Energy Policy Act (EP Act)   The Energy Policy Act of 1992 addresses a wide variety of energy issues. The legislation creates a new class of power generators, exempt wholesale generators (EWGs), that are exempt from the provisions of the Public Utilities Holding Company Act of 1935 and grants the authority to FERC to order and condition access by eligible parties to the interconnected transmission grid.

energy reserves The portion of total energy resources that is known and can be recovered with presently available technology at an affordable cost.

energy security/fuel security Policy that considers the risk of dependence on fuel sources located in remote and unstable regions of the world and the benefits of domestic and diverse fuel sources.

enthalpy The quantity of heat necessary to raise the temperature of a substance from one point to a higher temperature.

entitlement Electric energy or generating capacity that a utility has a right to access under power exchange or sales agreements.

Best Practice

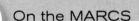

On the MARCS

In Ohio, the electric utility companies are integrating a multi-agency radio communications system (MARCS) into their line and service vehicles as well as dispatch system. The MARCS System is a state-wide radio system that allows for contiguous communications throughout the state. It will allow utility companies to know of and respond to power outages due to weather and other emergencies much more quickly and efficiently. Since utility companies can be fined heavily for extensive outages, this is also a cost-saving measure.

Environmental Protection Agency (EPA) A federal agency created in 1970 to permit coordinated governmental action for protection of the environment by systematic abatement and control of pollution through integration or research, monitoring, standards setting, and enforcement activities.

ESCO Efficiency Service Company, a company that offers to reduce a client's electricity consumption with the cost savings being split with the client.

ethanol A liquid that is produced chemically (from ethylene) or biologically (from the fermentation of various sugars from carbohydrates found in agricultural crops and cellulosic residues from crops or wood). Ethanol can also be used in higher concentration in vehicles optimized for its use.

ethylene A colorless gas that burns and is an oil refinery product.

exchange (electric utility) Agreements between utilities providing for purchase, sale, and trading of power. Usually relates to capacity (kilowatts), but sometimes energy (kilowatt-hours).

exempt wholesale generator (EWG)   Created under the 1992 Energy Policy Act, these wholesale generators are exempt from certain financial and legal restrictions stipulated in the Public Utilities Holding Company Act of 1935.

Federal Energy Regulatory Commission (FERC)   An independent regulatory commission within the U.S. Department of Energy that has jurisdiction over energy producers that sell or transport fuels for resale in interstate commerce.

firm energy   Power supplies that are guaranteed to be delivered under terms defined by contract.

fission   A release of energy caused by the splitting of an atom's nucleus. This is the energy process used in conventional nuclear power plants to make the heat needed to run steam electric turbines.

fissionable material   A substance whose atoms can be split by slow neutrons. Uranium-235, plutonium-239, and uranium-233 are fissionable materials.

flare gas   Unwanted natural gas that is disposed of by burning as it is released from an oil field.

flat plate   A device used to collect solar energy. It is a piece of metal painted black on the side facing the sun to absorb the sun's heat.

flexible fuel vehicle (FFV)   A vehicle that can operate on either alcohol fuels (methanol or ethanol) or regular unleaded gasoline or any combination of the two from the same tank.

flue gas   Gas that is left over after fuel is burned and which is disposed of through a pipe or stack to the outer air.

fluidized bed combustion   A process for burning powdered coal that is poured in a liquid-like stream with air or gases. The process reduces sulfur dioxide emissions from coal combustion.

forced air unit (FAU)   A central furnace equipped with a fan or blower that provides the primary means for circulation of air.

fossil fuel   Oil, coal, natural gas or their by-products; fuel that was formed in the Earth in prehistoric times from remains of living-cell organisms.

fractional distillation   The process of refining crude oil into various oil products.

frequency   The number of cycles that an alternating current moves through in each second. Standard electric utility frequency in the United States is 60 cycles per second, or 60 hertz.

fuel   A substance that can be used to produce heat.

fuel cell   A device or an electrochemical engine with no moving parts that converts the chemical energy of a fuel (such as hydrogen) and an oxidant (such as oxygen) directly into electricity.

fuel gas   Synthetic gas used for heating or cooling. It has less energy content than pipeline-quality gas.

fuel oil   Petroleum products that are burned to produce heat or power.

fuel reprocessing (nuclear)   The means for obtaining usable, fissionable material from spent reactor fuel.

fuel rod (nuclear)   A long slender tube that holds fissionable material (fuel) for nuclear reactor use. Fuel rods are assembled into bundles called fuel elements or assemblies, which are loaded individually into the reactor core.

fusion energy   A power source, now under development, based on the release of energy that occurs when atoms are combined under the most extreme heat and pressure. It is the energy process of the sun and the stars.

gas   Gaseous fuel (usually natural gas) that is burned to produce heat energy.

gas utility   Any person engaged in or authorized to engage in distributing or transporting natural gas, including, but not limited to, any such person who is subject to the regulation of the Public Utilities Commission.

gasification   The process of transforming materials that are primarily composed of carbon into a form of carbon monoxide and hydrogen that can be used as fuel.

gasohol   In the United States, gasohol (E10) refers to gasoline that contains 10 percent ethanol by volume.

gasoline   A light petroleum product obtained by refining oil, and used as motor vehicle fuel.

generating station   A power plant.

generation company (GENCO)   A regulated or non-regulated entity (depending upon the industry structure) that operates and maintains existing generating plants. The GENCO may own the generation plants or interact with the short-term market on behalf of plant owners.

generation dispatch and control   Aggregating and dispatching generation from various generating facilities, including providing backups and reliability services.

geothermal energy   Natural heat from within the Earth, captured for production of electric power, space heating, or industrial steam.

geothermal gradient   The change in the Earth's temperature with depth. As one goes deeper, the Earth becomes hotter.

geothermal steam   Steam drawn from deep within the Earth.

global climate change   Gradual changing of global climates due to buildup of carbon dioxide and other greenhouse gases in the Earth's atmosphere. Carbon dioxide produced by burning fossil fuels has reached levels greater than what can be absorbed by green plants and the seas.

greenhouse effect   When the presence of trace atmospheric gases make the Earth warmer than direct sunlight alone and certain gases absorb part of that energy before it escapes into space.

grid   The electric utility companies' transmission and distribution system that links power plants to customers through high power transmission line service.

H-coal process   A means of making coal cleaner so it will produce less ash and less sulfur emissions.

heat capacity   The amount of heat necessary to raise the temperature of a given mass one degree, calculated by multiplying the mass by the specific heat.

heat engine   An engine that converts heat to mechanical energy.

heat gain   An increase in the amount of heat contained in a space, resulting from direct solar radiation; heat flow through walls, windows, and other building surfaces; and the heat given off by people, lights, equipment, and other sources.

heating degree day   A unit that measure the space heating needs during a given period of time.

heating load   The rate at which heat must be added to a space in order to maintain the desired temperature within the space.

heating value   The amount of heat produced by the complete combustion of a given amount of fuel.

heat loss   A decrease in the amount of heat contained in a space, resulting from heat flow through walls, windows, roof and other building surfaces, and from ex-filtration of warm air.

heat pump   An air-conditioning unit which is capable of heating by refrigeration, transferring heat from one (often cooler) medium to another (often warmer) medium, and which may or may not include a capability for cooling.

heat rate   A number that tells how efficient a fuel-burning power plant is. The heat rate equals the Btu content of the fuel input divided by the kilowatt-hours of power output.

heat storm   Heat storms occur when temperatures exceed 100 degrees Fahrenheit over a large area for three days in a row.

heat transfer   Flow of heat energy induced by a temperature difference. Heat flow through a building envelope typically flows from a heated or hot area to a cooled or cold area.

heavy water   A type of hydrogen atom that may be used as fuel for fusion power plants.

hedging contracts   Contracts that establish future prices and quantities of electricity independent of the short-term market.

heliochemical   Using solar radiation to cause chemical reactions.

heliothermal   A process that uses the sun's rays to produce heat.

high-sulfur coal   Coal whose weight is more than one percent sulfur.

hot dry rock   A geothermal resource created when impermeable, subsurface rock structures—typically granite rock 15,000 feet or more below the Earth's surface—are heated by geothermal energy. The resource is being investigated as a source of energy production.

hybrid vehicle   A vehicle that employs a combustion engine system together with an electric propulsion system.

hydroelectric power   Electricity produced by falling water that turns a turbine generator.

hydroelectric spill generation   Hydroelectric generation that may have inadequate storage space.

hydronic heating   A system that heats a space using hot water, which may be circulated through a convection or fan coil system or through a radiant baseboard or floor system.

hydrothermal systems   Underground reservoirs that produce either dry steam or a mixture of steam and water.

hygas   A process that uses water to help produce pipeline-quality gas from coal.

imports (electric utility)   Power capacity or energy obtained by one utility from others under purchase or exchange agreement.

impoundment   A body of water confined by a dam, dike, floodgate or other artificial barrier.

independent power producer (IPP)   A producer that generates power purchased by an electric utility at wholesale prices. The utility then resells this power to end-use customers.

independent system operator (ISO)   A neutral operator responsible for maintaining instantaneous balance of the grid system. The ISO performs its function by controlling the dispatch of flexible plants to ensure that loads match resources available to the system.

infiltration   The uncontrolled inward leakage of air through cracks and gaps in the building envelope, especially around windows, doors, and duct systems.

injection (petroleum)   Forcing gas or water into an oil well to increase pressure and cause more oil to come to the surface.

integrated resource planning (IRP)   A public planning process and framework within which the costs and benefits of both demand- and supply-side resources are evaluated to develop the least-total-cost mix of utility resource options.

interchange (electric utility)   The agreement among interconnected utilities under which they buy, sell, and exchange power among themselves.

interconnection (electric utility)   The linkage of transmission lines between two utilities, enabling power to be moved in either direction. Interconnections allow the utilities to help contain costs while enhancing system reliability.

intertie   A transmission line that links two or more regional electric power systems.

joule   A unit of work or energy equal to the amount of work done when the point of application of force of 1 Newton is displaced 1 meter in the direction of the force. It takes 1,055 joules to equal a British thermal unit. It takes about 1 million joules to make a pot of coffee.

kerosene   Certain colorless, low-sulfur oil products that burn without producing much smoke.

landfill gas   Gas generated by the natural degrading and decomposition of municipal solid waste by anaerobic microorganisms in sanitary landfills.

latent heat   A change in the heat content that occurs without a corresponding change in temperature, usually accompanied by a change of state (as from liquid to vapor during evaporation).

latent load   The cooling load caused by moisture in the air.

lifeline rates   Rates charged by a utility company for the low-income, the disadvantaged, and senior citizens.

light water reactor (LWR)   A nuclear power unit that uses ordinary water to cool its core. The LWR may be a boiling water reactor or a pressurized water reactor.

lignite   Brownish black coal having qualities in between those of bituminous coal and peat. The texture of the original wood often is visible in lignite.

liquefaction   The process of making synthetic liquid fuel from coal. The term also is used to mean a method for making large amounts of gasoline and heating oil from petroleum.

liquefied gases   Gases that have been or can be changed into liquid form. These include butane, butylene, ethane, ethylene, propane, and propylene.

liquefied natural gas (LNG)   Natural gas that has been condensed to a liquid, typically by cryogenically cooling the gas to minus 260 degrees Fahrenheit (below zero).

liquefied petroleum gas (LPG)   A mixture of gaseous hydrocarbons, mainly propane and butane, that change into liquid form under moderate pressure. LPG or propane is commonly used as a fuel for rural homes for space and water heating, as a fuel for barbecues and recreational vehicles, and as a transportation fuel.

liquid brine   A type of geothermal energy resource that depends on naturally occurring hot water solution found within the Earth.

load   The amount of electric power supplied to meet one or more end-user's needs.

load centers   A geographical area where large amounts of power are drawn by end-users.

load diversity   The condition that exists when the peak demands of a variety of electric customers occur at different times.

load factor   A percent telling the difference between the amount of electricity a consumer used during a given time span and the amount that would have been used if the usage had stayed at the consumer's highest demand level during the whole time. The term also is used to mean the percentage of capacity of an energy facility, such as power plant or gas pipeline, that is utilized in a given period of time.

loading factor   Ratio of actual electricity consumed and total potential consumption, used when analyzing electricity consumption in a large population.

load management   Steps taken to reduce power demand at peak load times or to shift some of it to off-peak times. This may be with reference to peak hours, peak days, or peak seasons.

loop flow   The difference between scheduled and actual power flows on electric transmission lines.

losses (electric utility)   Electric energy or capacity that is wasted in the normal operation of a power system. Some kilowatt-hours are lost in the form of waste heat in electrical apparatus such as substation conductors.

low-sulfur coal   Coal having one percent or less of sulfur by weight.

low-sulfur oil   Oil having one percent or less of sulfur by weight.

luminaire   A complete lighting unit consisting of a lamp or lamps together with the parts designed to distribute the light, to position and protect the lamps, and to connect the lamps to the power supply.

M85   A blend of 85 percent methanol and 15 percent unleaded regular gasoline, used as a motor fuel.

M100   One hundred percent (neat) methanol used as a motor fuel in dedicated methanol vehicles, such as some heavy-duty truck engines.

magma   The molten rock and elements that lie below the Earth's crust. The heat energy can approach 1,000 degrees Fahrenheit and is generated directly from a shallow molten magma resource and stored in adjacent rock structures.

magneto hydro dynamics (MHD)   A means of producing electricity directly by moving liquids or gases through a magnetic field.

marketer   An agent for generation projects who markets power on behalf of the generator. The marketer may also arrange transmission or other ancillary services as needed.

market-based price   A price set by the mutual decisions of many buyers and sellers in a competitive market.

market clearing price   The price at which supply equals demand.

market participant   An entity, including a scheduling coordinator, who participates in the energy marketplace through the buying, selling, transmission, or distribution of energy or ancillary services into out of or through the ISO-controlled grid.

marsh gas A common term for gas that bubbles to the surface of the water in a marsh or swamp. It is colorless, odorless, and can be explosive.

methane A light hydrocarbon that is the main component of natural gas and marsh gas.

methanol A liquid formed by catalytically combining carbon monoxide (CO) with hydrogen (H2) in a 1:2 ratio, under high temperature and pressure. Also known as methyl alcohol, wood alcohol, CH3OH.

methyl tertiary butyl ether (MTBE) An ether manufactured by reacting methanol and isobutylene. The resulting ether has a high octane and low volatility.

minimum generation Generally, the required minimum generation level of a utility systems thermal units; specifically, the lowest level of operation of oil-fired and gas-fired units at which they can be currently available to meet peak load needs.

municipalization The process by which a municipal entity assumes responsibility for supplying utility service to its constituents. In supplying electricity, the municipality may generate and distribute the power or purchase wholesale power from other generators and distribute it.

municipal utility A provider of utility services owned and operated by a municipal government.

natural gas Hydrocarbon gas found in the Earth, composed of methane, ethane, butane, propane, and other gases.

natural gas vehicle Vehicles that are powered by compressed or liquefied natural gas.

natural gasoline A mixture of liquids extracted from natural gas and suitable for blending with ordinary oil-derived gasoline.

newton The amount of force it takes to accelerate one kilogram at one meter per second per second.

non-depletable energy sources Energy which is not obtained from depletable energy sources.

nuclear energy Power obtained by splitting heavy atoms (fission) or joining light atoms (fusion). A nuclear energy plant uses a controlled atomic chain reaction to produce heat. The heat is used to make steam run conventional turbine generators.

Nuclear Regulatory Commission (NRC) An independent federal agency that ensures that strict standards of public health and safety, environmental quality, and national security are adhered to by individuals and organizations possessing and using radioactive materials.

obligation to serve   The obligation of a utility to provide electric service to any customer who seeks that service, and is willing to pay the rates set for that service. Traditionally, utilities have assumed the obligation to serve in return for an exclusive monopoly franchise.

ocean thermal gradient (OTG)   Temperature differences between deep and surface water. Deep water is likely to be 25 to 45 degrees Fahrenheit colder.

octane   A rating scale used to grade gasoline as to its antiknock properties.

octane rating   A measure of a gasoline's resistance to exploding too early in the engine cycle, which causes knocking.

oil shale   A type of rock containing organic matter that produces large amounts of oil when heated to high temperatures.

Organization of the Petroleum Exporting Countries (OPEC)   An organization founded in 1960 to unify and coordinate petroleum polices of the members.

outage (electric utility)   An interruption of electric service that is temporary (minutes or hours) and affects a relatively small area (buildings or city blocks).

oxygenate   a term used in the petroleum industry to denote octane components containing hydrogen, carbon, and oxygen in their molecular structure.

ozone   A kind of oxygen that has three atoms per molecule instead of the usual two. Ozone is a poisonous gas, but the ozone layer in the upper atmosphere shields life on Earth from deadly ultraviolet radiation from space.

partial load   An electrical demand that uses only part of the electrical power available.

particulate matter (PM)   Unburned fuel particles that form smoke or soot and stick to lung tissue when inhaled.

passive solar energy   Use of the sun to help meet a building's energy needs by means of architectural design (such as arrangement of windows) and materials (such as floors that store heat, or other thermal mass).

peaking unit   A power generator used by a utility to produce extra electricity during peak load times.

peak load   The highest electrical demand within a particular period of time.

peak load power plant   A power generating station that is normally used to produce extra electricity during peak load times.

petrochemicals   Chemicals made from oil.

petrodollars   Money paid to other countries for oil imported to the United States.

petroleum   Oil as found it its natural state under the ground.

Petroleum Administration for Defense District (PADD) One of five regions in the United States, determined by the U.S. Department of Energy, utilized for research and planning purposes.

photocell   A device that produces an electric reaction to visible radiant energy (light).

photovoltaic cell   A semiconductor that converts light directly into electricity.

pipeline   A line of pipe with pumping machinery and apparatus (including valves, compressor units, metering stations, and regulator stations) for conveying a liquid or gas.

power authorities   Quasi-governmental agencies that perform all or some of the functions of a public utility.

power plant   A central station generating facility that produces energy.

power pool   Two or more interconnected utilities that plan and operate to supply electricity in the most reliable, economical way to meet their combined load.

pressurized water reactor (PWR)   A nuclear power unit cooled by water that is pressurized to keep it from boiling when it reaches high temperatures.

primary fuel   Fuel consumed in the original production of energy, before conversion takes place.

propane   A gas that is both present in natural gas and refined from crude oil. It is used for heating, lighting, and industrial applications.

pumped hydroelectric storage   Commercial method used for large-scale storage of power. During off-peak times, excess power is used to pump water to a reservoir. During peak times, the reservoir releases water to operate hydroelectric generators.

qualifying facility   A co-generator or small power producer that under federal law has the right to sell its excess power output to the public utility.

Problem
Solving

Seasonal Differences

During the winter heating season, power and natural gas companies regulated by the PUC must adhere to strict policies about shutting off power for nonpayment. Often when the temperature is very cold, below 20 degrees in many cases, disconnections for nonpayment are discontinued. Additionally, low-income consumers that qualify are able to make lower payments during the heating season. These special rules can be complicated and may change each heating season, which can impact customer service and the ability to comply. Some utility companies have solved this problem by creating new guidelines for special payment arrangements and disconnections prior to each heating season, then requiring all customer service representatives to attend a training session to go over them.

radiant energy   Energy transferred by the exchange of electromagnetic waves from a hot or warm object to one that is cold or cooler.

radiation   The flow of energy across open space via electromagnetic waves such as light; the passage of heat from one object to another without warming the air space in between.

radiation absorbed dose (RAD)   A unit of measure of absorbed radiation; one RAD equals 100 ergs (the unit of measure used to describe radiation exposure) of radiation energy per gram of absorbing material.

rate-basing   Refers to practice by utilities of passing on the costs of research, development, commercialization, and other programs to rate-payers in the form of a higher base rate charged on their bills, as opposed to allocating these costs to shareholders (by reducing dividends).

raw fuel   Coal, natural gas, wood, or other fuel that is used in the form in which it is found in nature, without chemical processing.

real-time pricing The instantaneous pricing of electricity based on the cost of the electricity available for use at the time the electricity is demanded by the customer.

recovered energy Reused heat or energy that otherwise would be lost. For example, a combined cycle power plant recaptures some of its own waste heat and reuses it to make extra electric power.

refinery A facility that separates crude oil into varied oil products.

reformulated gasoline (RFG) A cleaner-burning gasoline that has had its compositions and/or characteristics altered to reduce vehicular emissions of pollutants.

Regional Transmission Group (RTG) A voluntary organization of transmission owners, users, and other entities interested in coordinating transmission planning, expansion, operation, and use on a regional and inter-regional basis.

regulatory must-run generation Occurs when utilities are allowed to generate electricity when hydro resources are spilled for fish releases, irrigation, and agricultural purposes, and to generate power that is required by federal or state laws, regulations, or jurisdictional authorities.

renewable energy Resources that constantly renew themselves or that are regarded as practically inexhaustible. These include solar, wind, geothermal, hydro, and wood.

renewable resources Renewable energy resources are naturally replenished, but flow-limited. They are virtually inexhaustible in duration but limited in the amount of energy that is available per unit of time.

reserve The extra generating capability that an electric utility needs, above and beyond the highest-demand level required to meet its users' needs.

reserve generating capacity The amount of power that can be produced at a given point in time by generating units that are kept available in case of special need.

reserve margin The differences between the dependable capacity of a utility's system and the anticipated peak load for a specified period.

resistance (electrical) The ability of all conductors of electricity to resist the flow of current, turning some of it into heat. Resistance depends on the cross section of the conductor (the smaller the cross section, the greater the resistance) and its temperature (the hotter the cross section, the greater its resistance).

retorting   The heating of oil shale to remove oil.

self-generation   A generation facility dedicated to serving a particular retail customer, usually located on the customer's premises.

solar cell   A photovoltaic cell that can convert light directly into electricity. A typical solar cell uses semiconductors made from silicon.

solar collector   A component of an active or passive solar system that absorbs solar radiation to heat a transfer medium which, in turn, supplies heat energy to the space or water heating system.

solar energy   Heat and light radiated from the sun.

Solar Energy Research Institute (SERI)   Established in 1974 and funded by the federal government, the institute's general purpose is to support the U.S. Department of Energy;s solar energy program and foster the widespread use of all aspects of solar technology, including photovoltaics, solar heating and cooling, solar thermal power generation, wind ocean thermal conversion, and biomass conversion.

solar heat gain factor   An estimate used in calculating cooling loads of the heat gain due to transmitted and absorbed solar energy through 1/8-inch-thick, clear glass at a specific latitude, time, and orientation.

solar heating and hot water systems   Systems that provide two basic functions: (a) capturing the sun's radiant energy, converting it into heat energy, and storing this heat in insulated storage tank(s); and (b) delivering the stored energy as needed to either the domestic hot water or heating system.

solar irradiation   The amount of radiation, both direct and diffuse, that can be received at any given location.

solar power   Electricity generated from solar radiation.

solar radiation   Electromagnetic radiation emitted by the sun.

solar satellite power   A proposed process of using satellites in geosynchronous orbit above the Earth to capture solar energy with photovoltaic cells, convert it to microwave energy, beam the microwaves to Earth where they would be received by large antennas, and changed from microwave into usable electricity.

solar thermal   The process of concentrating sunlight on a relatively small area to create the high temperatures needed to vaporize water or other fluids to drive a turbine for generation of electric power.

solar thermal power plant   A plant that uses collected radiation from the sun to turn its turbines and create power.

source energy   All of the energy used in delivering energy to a site, including power generation and transmission and distribution losses, to perform a specific function, such as space conditioning, lighting, or water heating.

special contracts   Any contract that provides a utility service under terms and conditions beyond those listed in the utility's tariffs.

split-the-savings (electric utility)   The basis for settling economy-energy transactions between utilities. The added costs of the supplier are subtracted from the avoided costs of the buyer, and the difference is evenly divided.

steam electric plant   A power station that uses steam to turn the turbines, that in turn generates power. In most cases the steam us created when a fossil fuel is burned, or it could be created through a controlled nuclear reaction, through heat from the sun, or through the Earth's heat in a geothermal plant.

stranded benefits   Public interest programs and goals which could be compromised or abandoned by a restructured electric industry.

strategic petroleum reserve   Government-owned crude oil stockpiles stored at various locations in the Gulf Coast region of the country.

substation   A facility that steps up or steps down the voltage in utility power lines.

superconductor   A synthetic material that has very low or no electrical resistance. Such experimental materials are being investigated in laboratories to see if they can be created at near room temperatures.

supertanker   A very large ship designed to transport more than 500,000 deadweight tons of oil.

sustained orderly development   A condition in which a growing and stable market is identified by orders that are placed on a reliable schedule.

syncrude   Synthetic crude oil made from coal of from oil shale.

synfuel   Fuel that is artificially made as contrasted to that which is found in nature.

syngas   Synthetic gas made from coal.

thermal break (thermal barrier)   An element of low-heat conductivity placed in such a way as to reduce or prevent the flow of heat.

thermally enhanced oil recovery (TEOR)   Injection of steam to increase the amount of petroleum that may be recovered from a well.

thermal mass   A material used to store heat, thereby slowing the temperature variation within a space.

thermal power plant   Any stationary or floating electrical generating facility using any source of thermal energy, with a generating capacity of 50 megawatts or more.

thermal (energy) storage   A technology that lowers the amount of electricity needed for comfort conditioning during utility peak load periods.

tidal power   Energy obtained by using the motion of the tides to run water turbines that drive electric generators.

time-of-use meter   A measuring device that records the times during which a customer uses various amounts of electricity. This type of meter is used for customers who pay time-of-use rates.

time-of-use (TOU) rates   The pricing of electricity based on the estimated cost of electricity during a particular time block. Time-of-use rates are usually divided into three or four time blocks per 24-hour period (on-peak, mid-peak, off-peak and sometimes super off-peak) and by seasons of the year (summer and winter).

ton of cooling   A useful cooling effect equal to 12,000 Btu hours.

transfer (electric utility)   To move electric energy from one utility system to another over transmission lines.

transformer   A device used to transform alternating or intermittent electric energy in one circuit into energy of similar type in another circuit, commonly with altered values of voltage and current.

transmission   Transporting bulk power over long distances.

transmission-dependent utility   A utility that relies on its neighboring utilities to transmit to it the power it buys from its suppliers.

transmission owner An entity that owns transmission facilities or has firm contractual right to use transmission facilities.

transmitting utility (TRANSCO) This is a regulated entity which owns, and may construct and maintain, wires used to transmit wholesale power. It may or may not handle the power dispatch and coordination functions.

turbine generator A device that uses steam, heated gases, water flow, or wind to cause spinning motion that activates electromagnetic forces and generates electricity.

UA The amount of heat that could escape a specific building or other enclosure, like a car, when there is a one degree Fahrenheit temperature difference between the enclosure and the environment surrounding it.

ultrahigh voltage transmission Transporting electricity over bulk-power lines at voltages greater than 800 kilovolts.

unbundling Disaggregating electric utility service into its basic components and offering each component separately for sale with separate rates for each component.

universal service Electric service sufficient for basic needs (an evolving bundle of basic services) available to virtually all members of the population regardless of income.

uprate (electric utility) An increase in the rating or stated measure of generation or transfer capability.

upstream A term used in the petroleum industry referring to the exploration and production side of the business.

uranium A radioactive element, found in ores, of which atoms can be split to create energy.

uranium enrichment The process of increasing the percentage of pure uranium above the levels found in naturally occurring uranium ore so that it may be used as fuel.

utility A regulated entity that exhibits the characteristics of a natural monopoly. For the purposes of electric industry restructuring, "utility" refers to the regulated, vertically-integrated electric company.

utility distribution company (UDC) An entity that owns a distribution system for the delivery of energy to and from the ISO-controlled grid.

voltage of a circuit (electric utility) The electric pressure of a circuit, measured in volts.

volumetric wires charge A type of charge for using the transmission and/or distribution system that is based on the volume of electricity that is transmitted.

wet-bulb temperature   The temperature at which water, by evaporating into air, can bring the air to saturation at the same temperature. Wet-bulb temperature is measured by a wet-bulb psychrometer.

wheeling   The transmission of electricity by an entity that does not own or directly use the power it is transmitting. This term is often used colloquially as meaning "transmission".

wholesale competition   A system whereby a distributor of power would have the option to buy its power from a variety of power producers, and the power producers would be able to compete to sell their power to a variety of distribution companies.

wholesale power market   The purchase and sale of electricity from generators to resellers (who sell to retail customers) along with the ancillary services needed to maintain reliability and power quality at the transmission level.

wholesale transmission services   The transmission of electric energy sold, or to be sold, at wholesale in interstate commerce.

wires charge   A broad term that refers to charges levied on power suppliers or their customers for the use of the transmission or distribution wires.

xyloid coal   Brown coal or lignite mostly derived from wood.

Chapter 6

Resources

Thanks to the World Wide Web, more information is available to energy industry employees than ever before. From trade associations, Web sites, and publications, to schools and universities, there is a wealth of resources today that can give the employee a competitive edge and help him or her succeed in this exciting and fast-changing industry. These sources provide information such as job postings, news and information, research, the latest energy pricing, and pending industry laws and regulations. The difficulty lies in choosing the right sources. Once the employee determines a career path and area of specialization, resources supporting this choice are plentiful.

Here are some of the resources available today that focus on the energy industry or specific facets of it. Keep in mind, none of these listings are meant to be exhaustive or comprehensive. It is important for employees to conduct their own search for the resources that best fit their needs.

Associations and Organizations

While association fees can be expensive, the benefits of joining at least one can far exceed the costs involved (See Fast Facts, this section). The size of the organization's membership often determines the extent and quality of its benefits, but most associations offer continuing education, seminars, networking, and an annual conference.

They also usually keep up with the latest news and trends and seek to keep their members well informed. There are trade associations for every facet of the energy industry. Here some of the largest associations for energy professionals. Information has been provided by the associations' Web sites.

American Association of Petroleum Geologists includes geologists, geophysicists, CEOs, managers, consultants, students, and academicians involved in the petroleum industry and research. The purpose of the organization is to foster scientific research, advance the science of geology, promote technology, and inspire high professional conduct. AAPG was founded in 1917 and is currently the world's largest professional geological society. (http://www.aapg.org)

American Exploration and Production Council is a national trade association that represents 30 of the largest independent natural gas and crude oil exploration and production companies in the United States. AXPC members are "independent" in the sense that that they do not have petroleum refining or retail marketing operations and therefore are not integrated. They are generally publically-traded corporations. Most AXPC members also have international operations or interests. The AXPC mission is to work constructively for sound energy, environmental, and related public policies that encourage responsible exploration, development, and production of natural gas and crude oil to meet consumer needs and fuel the country's economy. (http://www.dpcusa.org)

American Gas Association was founded in 1918 and represents 199 local energy companies that deliver clean natural gas throughout the United States. There are more than 70 million residential, commercial, and industrial natural gas customers in the United States, of which 91 percent—more than 64 million customers—receive their gas from AGA members. Today, natural gas meets almost one-fourth of the United States' energy needs. The American Gas Association represents companies delivering natural gas to customers to help meet their energy needs. AGA members are committed to delivering natural gas safely, reliably, cost-effectively, and in an environmentally responsible way. AGA advocates the interests of its members and their customers, and provides information and services promoting the safe, reliable, and efficient delivery of natural gas. (http://www.aga.org)

American Petroleum Institute is the only national trade association that represents all aspects of America's oil and natural gas industry. Members come from all segments of the industry. They are producers, refiners, suppliers, pipeline operators and marine transporters, as well as service and supply companies that support all segments of the industry. The API provides its members with advocacy, research and statistics, standards, certification, and education. (http://api-ec.api.org)

American Public Gas Association is the only nonprofit trade organization representing America's publicly owned natural gas local distribution companies (LDCs). APGA represents the interests of public gas before congress, federal agencies, and other energy-related stakeholders. In addition, APGA organizes meetings, seminars, and workshops with a specific goal to improve the reliability, operational efficiency, and regulatory environment in which public gas systems operate. (http://www.apga.org)

American Wind Energy Association is a national trade association with more than 2,500 members and advocates, representing wind power project developers, equipment suppliers, services providers, parts manufacturers, utilities, researchers, and others involved in the wind industry. AWEA represents hundreds of wind energy advocates from around the world and provides up-to-date, accurate information about the domestic and international wind energy industry. (http://www.awea.org)

Association of Energy Engineers is a nonprofit professional society of more than 13,000 members in 81 countries. The mission of AEE is to promote the scientific and educational interests of those engaged in the energy industry and to foster action for sustainable development. AEE offers a full array of informational outreach programs including seminars (live and Internet-based), conferences, journals, books, and certification programs. (http://www.aeecenter.org)

Association of Energy Service Professionals is a member-based association dedicated to improving the delivery and implementation of energy efficiency, energy management, and distributed renewable resources. AESP provides professional development programs, a network of energy practitioners, and promotes the transfer of knowledge and experience. Members work in the energy services industry and represent electric and natural gas utilities, public benefits associations, regulatory and nonprofit entities, vendors, manufacturers, and consulting firms. (http://www.aesp.org)

The Energy Bar Association is a nonprofit voluntary association of attorneys, non-attorney professionals, and students, whose mission is to promote professional excellence and ethical integrity of its members in the practice, administration, and development of energy laws, regulations, and policies. The EBA is an international association of members active in all areas of energy law. It has approximately 2,600 members, six formal chapters across the United States and an increasing number of members across the United States and Canada. (http://www.eba-net.org)

Gas Processors Association has served the light hydrocarbons industry since 1921 as an incorporated nonprofit trade association. Its corporate members are engaged in the processing of

Keeping
in Touch

Networking: Create a New Mindset for Success

There is been a lot of hype about networking over the last several years, as well as tips and advice on how to do it "right." But experts all agree: it is a necessity. Some people, though just do not like doing it. Practicing and delivering a canned introduction and working the crowd can feel forced, phony, and like a lot of work. Today, experts say to lose the old mindset of looking for people that can help a career, and instead identify people that the employee can really connect with on a personal level. It's also important for the networking relationship to be equal—both sides should be able to help each other. Here are some benefits networking can provide when this approach is used:

- At the least, new friendships will be formed.
- Relationships with others interested in the industry can give the employee a new perspective.
- Connections with other companies in the energy industry.

natural gas into merchantable pipeline gas, volume movement, or
further processing of liquid products from natural gas. Member
companies represent approximately 92 percent of all natural gas
liquids produced in the United States and operate approximately
190,000 miles of domestic gas gathering lines. (http://www.gas-
processors.com)

Geological Society of America is a leader in advancing the geosciences, enhancing the professional growth of its members, and
promoting the geosciences in the service to humankind and
stewardship of the Earth. The GSA's growing membership unites
thousands of earth scientists from every corner of the globe in a
common purpose to study the mysteries of our planet and share
scientific findings. (http://www.geosociety.org)

Independent Petroleum Association of America represents the
thousands of independent oil and natural gas producers and service companies across the United States. Independent producers
develop 90 percent of domestic oil and gas wells, produce 68 percent of domestic oil, and produce 82 percent of domestic natural
gas. IPAA serves as an informed voice for the exploration and
production segment of the industry, and advocates its members'
views before the U.S. congress, administration, and federal agencies. IPAA provides economic and statistical information about
the domestic exploration and production industry. IPAA also
develops investment symposia and other opportunities for its
members. (http://www.ipaa.org)

National Association of Energy Service Companies is a national
trade association that has been promoting the benefits of the widespread use of energy efficiency for more than 25 years. On behalf
of its membership, NAESCO works to help open new markets for
energy services by directly promoting the value of demand reduction to customers through seminars, workshops, training programs,
publication of case studies and guidebooks, and the compilation
and dissemination of aggregate industry data. NAESCO represents
every facet of the energy services industry and is the industry's
advocate for the cost effective delivery of comprehensive energy
services to all customer classes. (http://www.naesco.org)

**National Council of Examiners for Engineering and Survey-
ing** is the place to go for all information about licensing requirements in the engineering and surveying professions. The Web site
contains a database of all contact information for state licensing
requirements, as well as suggestions to improve your credentials

and ace licensure examinations. Application for establishing a public work record—the quickest way to ensure interstate licensure—is also available. (http://www.ncees.org)

National Energy Marketers Association is a national, nonprofit trade association representing wholesale and retail marketers of natural gas, electricity, energy, and financial related products, services, information, and advanced technologies throughout the United States, Canada, and the European Union. NEM members are global leaders in the development of enterprise solution software for energy, advanced metering, information services, finance, risk management, and the trading of commodities and financial instruments. (http://www.energymarketers.com)

National Society of Professional Engineers has chapters at the national, state, and local level, making it easy for engineering professionals to network and trade ideas. The organization offers conferences, mentoring opportunities, professional development seminars, and other continuing education programs. (http://www.nspe.org/index.html)

Solar Energy Industry Association is for solar energy manufacturers, distributors, contractors, installers, project developers, consultants or in any other industry impacted by the U.S. solar energy market. SEIA provides its membership with critical information, advocacy, education, and networking opportunities designed to grow their businesses and ensure the long-term success of the solar industry. SEIA works to make solar a mainstream and significant energy source by expanding markets, removing market barriers, strengthening the industry, and educating the public on the benefits of solar energy. (http://www.seia.org/)

Books and Periodicals

Outfit yourself for your job search by delving into the literature of the industry, in both book and periodical form.

Books

Economics of the Energy Industries, Second Edition. By William Spanger Peirce (Source Book Publications, 1996). This is an excellent overview to the interrelation of energy and economics. Particularly relevant is its treatment of environmental issues and industry regulation.

On the Cutting Edge

Superconductors

Danko van der Laan, a University of Colorado scientist working at the National Institute of Standards and Technology (NIST), invented a method of making high-temperature superconducting (HTS) cables that are thinner and more flexible than the demonstration HTS cables currently installed in the electric power grid. Superconductors are materials that when cooled to a certain temperature lose a great deal of their electrical resistance, enabling electricity to flow with little to no loss of electricity. These new cables can carry the same amount of current, or even more. The compact cables could be used in the electric grid as well as scientific and medical equipment.

Electric Power Industry in Nontechnical Language. By Denise Warkentin-Glenn (Kindle Books, 2006). In layman's terms, author Warkentin-Glenn addresses the history and recent developments of the electric power industry. She covers information on utilities, merchant plants, rural cooperatives, and government entities, as well as the 2005 Energy Policy Act, environmental standards, and the nuances of recent industry mergers and acquisitions.

From Edison to Enron: The Business of Power and What it Means for the Future of Electricity. By Richard Munson (Praeger, 2005). A thorough introduction to the electric power industry, featuring in-depth profiles of many of the inventors, businessmen, and others who helped shape the world of electricity.

Green Careers in Energy: Your Guide to Jobs in Renewable Energy. (Peterson's, 2010). This guidebook to the burgeoning green energy sector highlights the most promising job opportunities, including solar, wind, geothermal, hydroelectric and marine, biofuel, and hydrogen.

Oil 101. By Morgan Downey (Wooden Table Press, 2009). A comprehensive overview of the oil industry, dubbed an "industry must-read" by the *Financial Times.*

Solar Revolution: The Economic Transformation of the Global Energy Industry. By Travis Bradford (The MIT Press, 2006). Fund manager and former corporate buyout specialist Travis Bradford makes the case for solar power's ascent over the next two decades. He argues that solar energy will increasingly become the best and cheapest choice for most electricity and energy applications, and outlines the path by which the transition to solar technology and sustainable energy practices will occur.

Understanding Today's Electricity Business. By Bob Shively and John Ferrare (Enerdynamics LLC, 2010). This is a straightforward introduction to the electricity industry, from the physical components of electrical systems to the major industrial players and common business models.

Wind Energy in the 21st Century: Economics, Policy, Technology and the Changing Electricity Industry. By Robert Y. Redlinger, Per Dannemand Andersen, and Poul Erik Morthorst (Palgrave Macmillan, 2001). This book follows the rise of wind energy from the energy crisis of the 1970s through the present day. It covers the current economic, financial, technical, environmental, competitive, and policy considerations facing the wind energy industry, and the means of going forward as outlined by various industry professionals.

Periodicals

Many of these magazines and journals are published by industry associations or scientific organizations. Information about them has been provided by the periodical's Web site.

American Gas magazine is published monthly by the American Gas Association. Its goal is to provide information to natural gas industry professionals that can enhance their effectiveness and companies' effectiveness.   (http://www.aga.org/Newsroom/magazine/Pages/default.aspx)

Annual Review of Environment and Resources provides reviews of significant topics within environmental science and engineering, including ecology and conservation science, water and energy resources, atmosphere, and energy technology innovation. (http://www.annualreviews.org/journal/energy)

Cogeneration and Distributed Generation Journal is one of three publications produced by the American Association of Energy

Engineers. This 80-page quarterly journal provides detailed information and expert analysis of the power market to help engineers make decisions for their companies. Contributions from leading authorities cover the full spectrum of both technical and non-technical issues, from financial and regulatory trends, to cogeneration and distributed generation success stories. (http://aeecenter.metapress.com/app/home/about.asp)

Cogeneration & On-Site Power Production magazine focuses on the clean and highly-efficient generation of power through decentralized generation and combined heat and power for an industrial, utility, and governmental audience. The magazine is published in association with the World Alliance for Decentralized Energy (WADE). (http://www.omeda.com)

Distributed Energy says it is the journal of energy efficiency and reliability. It provides news and the latest information on technologies for energy distributors. The publication addresses the concerns of readers regarding the vulnerability of their operations and facilities to power interruptions, and explores solutions for increasing energy self-reliance. (http://www.distributedenergy.com)

Earth, published by the American Geological Institute, is dedicated to providing the latest news and information on the Earth, energy, and environment. (http://www.earthmagazine.org)

Electric Energy magazine is published six times a year and serves the fields of electric utilities, investor owned, rural, and other electric cooperatives, municipal electric utilities, independent power producers, electric contractors, wholesalers and distributors of electric utility equipment, manufacturers, major power consuming industries, consulting engineers, state and federal regulatory agencies and commissions, industry associations, communication companies, oil and gas companies, universities, and libraries. (http://www.electricenergyonline.com)

Electricity Today is a leading electrical transmission and distribution magazine distributed free of charge to North American transmission and distribution electric utility engineering, construction, and maintenance personnel, and high voltage transmission and distribution consulting engineers. (http://www.electricity-today.com)

Enerfax Daily provides the latest prices in the natural gas and oil market, as well as the latest news and information for the power and gas industry. (http://www.enerfaxdaily.com)

Energy Engineering Journal is published by the Association of Energy Engineers. This journal contains expert commentary on technological developments in such areas as energy management, HVAC and building systems, energy-efficient products, combustion technologies, distributed generation, thermal storage, load management, Internet energy management, gas cooling, geo-exchange, cogeneration, fuel cells, energy procurement, lighting, utility deregulation, engineering, energy policy, and more. (http://aeecenter.metapress.com/app/home/about.asp)

Energy Law Journal is produced by the Energy Bar Association. It is published twice a year for members of the association and affiliated readers. The journal covers international as well as domestic energy topics, laws, regulations, and government policies that impact the energy industry. (http://www.felj.org/journal_vol31-22010.php)

Environmental Geosciences Journal is a quarterly publication produced by the American Association of Petroleum Geologists. The journal approaches basic environmental issues from a geological perspective, thereby transferring the profession's understanding of geological, geochemical, geophysical, and hydrogeological principles and methodologies to the solutions of environmental problems. (http://deg.aapg.org/journal.cfm)

Power Engineering Magazine is a monthly engineering and applications magazine that serves the North American power generation industry including electric utilities, industrial power plants, independent power producers, co-generators, and the engineering design and construction firms serving this industry. (http://www.omeda.com/poe)

The Source, published by the American Public Gas Association, delivers timely information and analysis on energy issues and policies that will impact customers served by community-owned gas utilities. From safety to the price end-users pay, from available gas supply to appliance efficiency, from climate change to the carbon footprint of communities served by gas utilities, the magazine's goal is to keep readers current on issues that impact community-owned gas systems and offer ideas to improve overall system operations. (http://www.apga.org/i4a/pages/index.cfm?pageid=3303)

Web Sites

Web sites can offer energy industry professionals and employees more than just up-to-date information. Websites are a great way for employees to network with others in the industry through bulletin boards, blogs, and similar forms of communication. If one person is experiencing a problem, he or she can seek the advice of others—something that can't be done using other resources.

Into the Wind, the blog site of the American Wind Energy Association, provides insights, comments, and opinions of professionals working in the wind energy industry. The blog also offers the latest wind energy news. There is no registration required to access the blog. (http://www.aweablog.org)

Bloomberg's energy page is free and requires no membership or registration. Its primary goal is to provide the latest pricing on oil gas (heating oil and gasoline), natural gas, and electricity. (http://www.bloomberg.com/energy)

Electricity Forum focuses on electricity news and power industry information. It is dedicated to the exchange of policy and technical information about electricity and electrical energy matters. Site content deals with issues in common to electric utilities and large industrial, commercial, and institutional power consumers. The site also provides listings of industry conferences, training courses, jobs, and other resources. (http://www.electricityforum.com)

ElectricNet publishes the latest news, research, and developments in the electric industry. It also provides a forum where electric industry buyers and sellers can come together. ElectricNet also offers tools, resources, and a free newsletter to subscribers. (http://www.electricnet.com)

Emerging Markets Online is a market research publisher and strategic investment and market advisory services firm serving the needs of clients in biofuels, oil, gas, government, R&D, and economic development initiatives. The site publishes conference and certification information, as well as biofuel industry news. Interested professionals will need to purchase the industry research and market forecasts, but other information is free. (http://www.emerging-markets.com)

Energy Central is a resource for the global power industry. It publishes the latest news in the energy industry, a calendar of webcasts, conferences, and shows and job listings for energy professionals. Research reports are also available for purchase and white papers, case studies, and a directory of associations and trade organizations are also available. Professionals can also subscribe to the site's e-news and updates. (http://www.energy-central.com)

Energy Markets provides links to other resources available to energy industry professionals. Resources for energy, fuel, gasoline, natural gas, and oil industries appear on the site. (http://www.energy-markets.com)

Energy User News is an information site geared toward the end-user. Information on the various types of energy appears on the site. The energy industries/topics covered include renewable, photovoltaic, solar, wind, green, alternative, and nuclear energy. Articles discuss efficiency, lighting, cleanliness, and other subjects important to consumers today. (http://www.energyusernews.com)

EnergyWeb is divided into different energy industry segments: oil, renewable energy, petrochemicals, gas, mining, power/electricity, subsea, energy conservation, floating production, and ocean technology. There is a directory companies can use and listings are free. There are also listings of events and publications, and readers can subscribe to the EnergyWeb newsletter at no charge. (http://www.energyweb.net/default.asp)

Educational Institutions

Getting ahead in the energy industry will take more than networking. This is a very technical industry, and even professionals in marketing, human resources, and other related positions should have a good grasp of the technology their company uses to provide service to customers. Employees also need to keep up with the latest knowledge, skills, and certifications in the industry. Continuing education is important in every field, but especially so in the rapidly changing energy industry.

Over the last five years, many schools, colleges, or universities have begun to respond to the energy industry's call for programs designed to educate and train potential employees. Many of these programs are designed to train technicians and are offered by technical schools and community colleges. However, a growing number of universities are also launching bachelor degree programs and post-graduate programs to provide the industry with engineers, researchers, and executives. Below is a list and description of some of the top programs in the country. All information has been taken from the school, college, or university Web site unless otherwise noted.

California Wind Tech provides an entry level training for wind technicians, wind industry professionals, and technical representatives. In order to meet the growing demand for a workforce trained in wind turbine systems, the California Wind Tech offers a monthly course that is both fast paced and filled with specialized information. Students receive a certificate for their coursework. (http://www.californiawindtech.com)

Cerro Cosso Community College offers an industrial technology associate's degree that is designed to prepare students to enter the industrial setting in the areas of renewable energy (wind/solar), engineering technology, or electronics. Within the program, students can earn progressive levels of certificates toward employment and/or the degree. Students participating in Cerro Cosso's program are required to complete 18 units of part-time coursework spread out over 1 year of classes. (http://www.cerrocoso.edu)

Columbia Gorge Community College began its renewable energy technology training program, focusing on wind technician training, in January 2007. The curriculum was designed with direct and continuing industry guidance and is supported in part by wind industry partners. The RET program now offers a one-year certificate and two-year associate's degree. (http://www.cgcc.cc.or.us)

Illinois State University offers a bachelor of science degree in renewable energy. Students are able to choose between two tracks: a technology track or an economics/public policy track. Graduates will be prepared for jobs in the fields of biofuels, wind and solar energy, or regulatory and governmental agencies. The program is designed to prepare students to enter an emerging field with employment opportunities across a variety of industries including biofuels, solar, wind, regulatory, and government agencies. Graduates are expected to be conversant in diverse disciplines, including technical, managerial, political, and economic issues important to renewable energy. (http://tec.illinoisstate.edu)

John Brown University offers a renewable energy program designed to provide students with a bachelor of science degree in renewable energy. Students are required to choose one of three emphasis areas: design, international development, or management. Students in the major are required to take a core number of about half a dozen classes, and then they take courses that develop their respective areas of emphasis. (http://www.jbu.edu/majors/renewable_energy)

Lake Area Technical Institute offers programs in energy operations and energy technology, including coursework in mechanical maintenance, repair, and overhaul, as well as alignment techniques, metallurgy, pneumatics, hydraulics, thermodynamics, combustion, vibration analysis, and dynamic balancing. (http://www.lakeareatech.edu)

Lorain County Community College offers an associate's degree in alternative energy technology, with a focus on wind turbines. The degree will train students to become installation and maintenance professionals. The program will covers an overview of

Fast Facts

Why Join?

Why should you join an energy industry trade association? Here's a list of the top reasons why joining one might be a great career move:

- Networking: Meet people who can help you move up the ladder or connect you with jobs and other resources you need.

- Information: Most associations publish newsletters, journals, or magazines with the latest industry news, trends, and technologies. Many also offer seminars and conferences led by key leaders in the field.

- Education: Many associations offer continuing education, training, and certifications.

- Advocacy: The energy industry is highly regulated. Large associations often employ top lobbyists who advocate for new laws or revisions to existing ones that impact the industry.

- Jobs: Several associations offer job boards, postings, or other employment services.

alternative energy sources, with specialized training in electronics, electronic controls, mechanical systems, and more. (http://www.lorainccc.edu)

Mid-State Technical College is one of the first in the country to offer students associate's degree programs in renewable energy careers. Current programs available include biorefinery technology, energy efficiency technician, renewable electricity technician, renewable energy specialist, and renewable thermal energy technician. (http://www.mstc.edu)

Minnesota West Community and Technical College offers an associate's degree program for energy technical specialists. This degree conveys the skills and knowledge necessary to be successful in the traditional and renewable energy fields. The degree will prepare students for work as technicians in the following industries: coal-fired electric power generation, natural gas distribution, ethanol production, biodiesel production, wind turbine maintenance, and solar energy. (http://www.mnwest.edu)

Mitchell Technical Institute offers training programs in energy production and transmission. A large focus of these programs is gaining hands on experience under the supervision of experienced technicians. Programs include power line construction and maintenance, propane and natural gas technologies, power line utility technologies, and wind turbine technology. (http://www.mitchelltech.edu)

Northwest Energy Education Institute offers both standard and custom learning opportunities throughout the northwest for practicing professionals in the energy industry, including an energy management certification program. NEEI has provided energy efficiency training and development throughout the northwest region since 1998. Participants have included technicians, contractors, engineers, architects, consultants, utility personnel, and energy managers. The NEEI is located on the campus of Lane Community College. (http://www.nweei.org)

Northwest Renewable Energy Institute offers green energy training programs that teach students the technical skills necessary to service, repair, and maintain the demanding requirements of wind turbines. (http://www.nw-rei.com)

Oregon Institute of Technology offered the first bachelor of science degree in renewable energy in North America. Electrical and mechanical engineering fundamentals, combined with upper-division coursework in energy-specific classes, prepare graduates for careers in the energy sector in general, and renewable energy in particular. (http://www.oit.edu)

University of Delaware's Institute of Energy Conversion is a laboratory devoted to research and development of thin-film photovoltaic solar cells and other photonic devices. Professional staff members jointly supervise graduate students for masters and doctorate degrees in conjunction with the departments of chemical engineering, electrical engineering, materials science, mechanical engineering, and physics. Students must apply through the academic department of their choosing at the University of Delaware. (http://www.udel.edu/iec)

University of Massachusetts–Lowell offers a graduate program in energy engineering that offers professional training at the master's degree level designed to prepare the student to perform state-of-the-art work on energy systems. There are two options: renewable (solar) engineering, and nuclear engineering. The University of Massachusetts also offers a doctoral program in energy engineering, which is designed to prepare engineers for leadership positions in industry, academia, and government and to provide society with sustainable energy systems. Presently the two areas of concentration are the same as the master's program, renewable (solar) and nuclear. (http://energy.caeds.eng.uml.edu)

Index

Elgin Community College
Library